Pirates
of the North Atlantic

W9-BTR-878

William S. Crooker
author of *Oak Island Gold*

Copyright © 2004 William S. Crooker

All rights reserved. No part of this book may be reproduced, stored in a retrieval system or transmitted in any form or by any means without the prior written permission from the publisher, or, in the case of photocopying or other reprographic copying, permission from Access Copyright, 1 Yonge Street, Suite 1900, Toronto, Ontario M5E 1E5.

Nimbus Publishing Limited
PO Box 9166
Halifax, NS B3K 5M8
(902) 455-4286

Printed and bound in Canada
Design: Kathy Kaulbach, Paragon Design Group
Visit the author's website at: www.oakislandgold.com

Library and Archives Canada Cataloguing in Publication

        Crooker, William S.
        Pirates of the North Atlantic / William S. Crooker.
        ISBN 1-55109-513-0

1. Pirates--North Atlantic Ocean—History. I. Title.
F106.C76 2004   910.4'5   C2004-906362-6

The Canada Council | Le Conseil des Arts
for the Arts | du Canada

We acknowledge the financial support of the Government of Canada through the Book Publishing Industry Development Program (BPIDP) and the Canada Council for our publishing activities.

For my wife, Joan

Acknowledgements

My wife, Joan, deserves my sincere thanks and appreciation for her unselfish endurance of my remoteness while I wrote this book, and for always being there when I needed her to read a story with a critical eye.

Thanks also to Chris Webb, for taking the time to hear my ideas and searching out many good sources for research, and Dan Soucoup, for all his encouragement while I was writing, and for providing excellent sources of information.

The staff of the Keshen Goodman branch of the Halifax Public Libraries provided excellent assistance with word processing problems and further helped by acquiring copies of books long out of print. Also thanks to the staff of the Nova Scotia Archives for helping me retrieve vital information.

Preface

Several years before I wrote this book, my publisher spoke with me about the remarkable absence of books about piracy off the east coast of North America, and particularly off the shores of Atlantic Canada. He noted that the "romance of piracy" seems to relate to the West Indies: When most people reflect on piracy, they see swashbucklers anchored off a tropical island, drinking rum in the shade of a palm tree, burying a treasure chest in the sands of a plush creamy beach, or battling a Spanish galleon in the heat of the southern sun. But some of the most feared pirates preyed heavily on shipping off the east coast of Canada and the Unites States, and pillaged defenceless villages in the bays and harbours of the western North Atlantic.

My publisher was aware of the piratical activity that had taken place on the western side of the North Atlantic and asked if I would be interested in writing a book about pirates of eastern North America, especially Atlantic Canada. I certainly was interested, but for various reasons it was not until the spring of 2003 that I found time to begin *Pirates of the North Atlantic*.

My first task before beginning the research and writing was to single out the pirates who stood out above the many who pillaged and plundered along the North American east coast— to line up the most notorious, depraved, and interesting, as time and space did not permit coverage of all. For example, Edward Low was more fiendish and cruel than any other pirate in the annals of piratical history; William Kidd is virtually the symbol of piracy although there is evidence that he was a privateer only and never a pirate; Peter Easton, an English gentleman, retired to the French Riviera an exceedingly wealthy man, and adopted the title of Marquis of Savoy; Henry Mainwarring, a lawyer, scholar, politician, soldier, and mariner, retired from piracy, was knighted, and rose up through the ranks of the Royal Navy to the position of Vice Admiral; and Edward and Margaret Jordan were a husband and wife team.

As with all stories obscured by time, there are probably inaccuracies in my accounts, but there are also many well-documented events. I studied numerous references, rejecting and accepting them according to their credibility.

Writing this volume was a pleasure. It has always been my objective to entertain as well as inform, and I truly hope that you enjoy reading this book as much as I enjoyed writing it.

W. S. C.

Table of Contents

Introduction

In the seventeenth, eighteenth, and even into the nineteenth centuries, pirates pilfered and plundered the east coast of North America, from the Carolinas to Newfoundland, and as far east as the islands of the Azores. These bloody rovers of the sea were, to large extent, the result of the reoccurring wars between England and her major adversaries, France and Spain. None of the countries had a powerful navy, so they enlisted privateers, who carried letters of marque licensing them to capture enemy ships, to help fight their wars. But when a war ended, a privateer captain and his crew had nowhere to turn but piracy.

Commonly defined, a pirate is a man or woman who once engaged in the practice of robbing vessels on the high seas during the age of wooden ships. (In our age, of course, a pirate may have no connection with the sea. Illegally copying computer software, for instance, is referred to as piracy.) The pirates of this book are the sea brigands of the days of wooden ships. They are the most romanticized figures of the world's seven seas. Rather than work for meagre seaman's wages, pirates shared in the spoils of plunder, and some retired in very favourable circumstances. They were engaged in a very dangerous profession, however, and if they weren't killed or severely wounded in battle, they stood the chance of being arrested for piracy, the penalty for which was death by hanging.

During the centuries of colonization of the New World, the English decided that even when at peace with Spain, they were not obliged to adhere to any peace treaty with respect to the Spanish colonies in the West Indies. This gave rovers of the deep the opportunity to prey on Spanish galleons en route to Spain from the Caribbean, carrying enormous loads of gold, gems and precious jewels stripped from the Maya, Aztec and Inca empires.

The route that the Spanish treasure ships took to Spain from the Caribbean usually followed the Gulf Stream up the eastern coast of North America, to a latitude north of Bermuda where westerly winds assisted in the homeward journey. On this course, the Spanish convoys often came within three or four hundred miles of Nova Scotia. Pirates of the eastern Atlantic seaboard, like Peter Easton, preyed on these shipments of unimaginable value, much to the distress of Spain.

But even without Spanish treasure ships, Newfoundland was a gold mine to pirates. Over ten thousand people with about four hundred ships were engaged in the gigantic fishing industry there; the waters teemed with fish, which were caught, salted and dried. A shipload sold for the equivalent of millions of dollars in today's market. A pirate captain and his crew who managed to capture a loaded fishing vessel en route to Europe from Newfoundland could sell the ship and cargo at one of the many free ports of France where a huge black market carried out a brisk trade with Muslim kingdoms of North Africa.

People generally perceive pirates as cruel and evil, but piracy was not always a personal choice. Many wanted very much *not* to be part of the piratical fraternity. Men were frequently forced to join a pirate crew to save their own lives. An honest, hard-working seaman would be on a commercial vessel when it was captured by pirates and his capabilities and skills assessed. If he were a physician or a carpenter, and ships were for ever in need of both, there was little chance of escaping death if he refused to join. Indeed, most capable seaman had no choice but to sign on.

Female pirates were far less likely to be pressed into service— they were often not welcome aboard at all. Still, there were enough of these women to leave a strong piratical legacy. Princess Alwida, daughter of a Gothic king, avoided an arranged marriage with Prince Alf, son of a Danish king, by adopting the life of a sea brigand. She joined an all-female pirate crew that dressed as men, and proved her worth as a ferocious pirate. In the early 1800s, Mrs. Ching, a Chinese lady pirate terrorized Europeans to the point where her name became an icon for a woman pirate. And Mary Read, an Englishwoman and ferocious pirate, fooled hundreds of pirates into believing she was a man.

Unfortunately, there are few confirmed cases of these "lady pirates" in the waters of the North Atlantic, and thus, with the exception of Margaret Jordan, female pirates are not represented in these pages.

John Phillips,
the Newfoundland Fish Splitter

How a

dreary job

led this man

to piracy,

plunder, and

a violent

death.

John Phillips, Newfoundland fish-splitter, sliced the razor-sharp blade down the stomach of his last creature of the sea to be cut that day. Wiping the knife blade clean of fish scales and blood on a filthy piece of canvas, he tossed it on a low shelf below the cutting table where it landed among a cluster of identical knives, all to be sharpened by others before the next eighteen hours of boring labour.

Phillips, an Englishman from a family of shipwrights, expected more from life than to spend his days splitting fish—a job that just paid for food and lodging and a ration of rum in return for intolerably long hours of drudgery. He had started his working life over in England as a carpenter's helper at a young age, about twelve years old. Parents forced their children to help pay the landlord and put bread and butter on the table. The carpenter's trade in the shipwright industry wasn't great, but far exceeded cleaning out the innards of cod. At that point of his life, however, he knew no worse job than carpentry, and had grown tired of sawing boards and hammering nails. In the local pub he heard sailors tell thrilling stories of their lives at sea as men who had travelled talked of all the fun they had experienced across the Atlantic in the new country. There was particularly talk about Newfoundland—ships regularly sailed back and forth between English ports and Newfoundland. It was the place to go! He had spent nights dreaming of a change of pace, an adventure abroad. Something he could later recount in the pubs to attentive crowds.

In 1720, a few years after entering the carpentry trade, Phillips decided to set out in search of a better, more exciting life. There would be an opportunity in the shipyard trade across the sea. England had taken over the shipyards in Placentia, a coastal settlement in Newfoundland, from France under the treaty of 1713, and was said to be operating a booming business. So he packed his bags and signed on a ship bound for Newfoundland.

The cruise had been relatively uneventful until one day out on the Grand Banks, not far from Newfoundland, when his ship was attacked by the sadistic pirate Anstis, one of the most depraved in the history of piracy. Anstis had a reputation for throwing his captives overboard, impressing o nly those that could fill a vacancy in his crew; captured women were raped and murdered. Carpenters were always needed, so Phillips was spared and signed pirate articles.

Not long after Phillips was taken aboard, Anstis captured the ship *Irwin*, commanded by a Captain Ross. In this undertaking, Phillips's introduction to the career of piracy could not have been more shocking. He witnessed the brutal gang-rape and murder of a female passenger, which ended with her being thrown overboard to the sharks.

Following this violent capture of the *Irwin*, Anstis and his pirates decided to apply to the British Crown for a pardon. They signed what was known as a "round-robin," a circle of signatures placing no one at the top of the list. Pirates frequently used this method to appeal to the British government for clemency, so noone bore any more responsibility than anyone else for the crimes committed.

Pardon was granted and Phillips returned to England on a merchant ship; he then signed on another, bound for Newfoundland, and arrived at Placentia in the spring of 1723, three years after he first attempted to reach the colony. But the work situation in the shipwright industry at Placentia wasn't as promised. Phillips was unable to find work as a shipwright in that location, so he went down to the island now called St. Pierre and Miquelon, off the southern coast of Newfoundland, in search of work as a carpenter or shipwright. He was not able to find the work of his trade there, either, and was obliged to take the fish-splitting job that he found so loathsome.

During his days of fish-splitting, Phillips became well acquainted with sixteen other men who had the same job. They, too, hated every moment of the monotonous work. Phillips talked with them about his experience as a pirate and soon sold them on the idea of forming a pirate band.

With Phillips as leader, plans were made to steal a ship anchored in the St. Pierre harbour. It was a trading schooner owned by William Minot of Boston. The night of August 29, 1723 was chosen for the heist, but when Phillips arrived at the predetermined meeting place on the shore only four of the sixteen had shown up. Phillips was determined not to go back to fish-splitting and decided to carry out the theft despite the shortage of manpower. They appropriated the schooner and sailed out of the harbour, with no one in pursuit.

The next day, when safely out at sea, Phillips renamed the stolen schooner: he called her the *Revenge*. Then he proceeded to draw up pirate articles for the ship. First was the matter of the division of spoils. It read: "The Captain shall have one full share and a half in all Prizes; the Master, Carpenter, Boatswain, and Gunner shall have one Share and quarter." Next, was the matter of loyalty: "If any Man shall offer to run away, or keep any Secret from the Company, he shall be maroon'd, with one Bottle of Powder, one bottle of Water, and one small Arm and Shot." Theft was a concern: "If any Man shall steal any Thing in the Company, or game to the Value of a Piece of Eight, he shall be maroon'd or shot." One of the items was rare for any ship of the day because it amounted to something akin to modern-day insurance: "If any man shall lose a Joint in Time of an Engagement, he shall have 400 Pieces of Eight, if a Limb, 800." In view of what he had witnessed while serving under Anstis, Phillips understandably did not omit an article related to rape. This article read: "If at any Time we meet with a prudent Woman, that Man that offers to meddle with her, without her Consent, shall suffer present Death." There was included an article pertaining to good behaviour that stipulated, "That man that shall strike another whilst these Articles are in force, shall receive Moses' Law (that is, 40 Stripes lacking one) on the bare Back." Phillips and the four men who showed up that night of the heist signed the articles. Their names and ranks were: John Phillips, captain; John Nutt, navigator; Thomas Fern, carpenter; James Sparks, gunner; and William White, crewmember.

Although the crew was tiny at the outset, it soon grew as Phillips captured ships and gathered men who either willingly joined or were impressed because of their special skills. One captured man stood out above the rest. He was the infamous pirate John Rose Archer, who had once served as Blackbeard's lieutenant. Phillips appointed him ship's quartermaster. Another noteworthy recruit was John Fillmore, whose grandson, Millard Fillmore, became the thirteenth president of the United States of America.

For several months, Phillips proceeded to run down and capture ships on the Grand Banks of Newfoundland. Among the ships captured on the Grand Banks, special mention is made of two: *Mary*, commanded by a Captain Moor and carrying a cargo valued at five hundred pounds, and a French vessel carrying over a thousand gallons of wine and valuable supplies.

Leaving the Grand Banks for warmer climes, Phillips sailed down to the West Indies, but found few ships to loot; trade had badly dried up in the region. The *Revenge* did, however, fall in with a French sloop from Martinique which gave them no resistance although it had twelve deadly guns. Phillips plundered the vessel, took on much-needed provisions, and let it sail away. Then he headed for the island of Tobago to work on the *Revenge*. The hull was badly covered with sea growth, so he ran the ship up on shore at high tide for careening. This work was done in a beautiful little cove with a white sand beach, a plush jungle growing down to its back edge, and abundant fresh potable water.

Here at Tobago they captured a small vessel and began fitting it for piratical venture. It was a comfortable little ship and Thomas Fern, one of the original founders of Phillips' pirate band, conspired with four of the crew to steal it and go off on their own. Fern had been holding a grudge against Phillips for some time for appointing John Archer rather than himself as ship's quartermaster, and was happy with the opportunity to part company with Phillips.

It was the month of February 1724. Phillips finished work on the ships and set a course northerly, with Fern in command of the recently captured small ship. Not long after putting out to sea, Fern began lagging behind the *Revenge* and, when he thought the moment was right, began to run away. But Phillips had a watchful eye, saw what Fern was up to, and gave chase.

Fern almost got away, but the wind stopped blowing in his favour and Phillips caught up with him. Fern and his fellow conspirators were taken aboard the *Revenge* and Phillips held a trial. He gave Fern the severest of the two penalties for theft named in the ship's articles: one day while on shore, Fern was tied to a tree and shot through the heart. The four other men of the conspiracy were pardoned and returned to serve with the crew. It is not clear why they were not found guilty of disobeying the ship's article pertaining to running away or keeping a secret from the "Company." Perhaps history is incorrect and they were innocent of any wrongdoing, simply obeying the skipper's orders; or perhaps they convinced Phillips of their innocence.

Fern's capture was not without a skirmish: Fern fired his pistol at Phillips and missed, one man was killed, and another man was shot in the leg. This last injury was so severe that the limb had to be amputated. There was no surgeon among the crew, so the carpenter was chosen to hack off the leg. He went below and came back with the largest saw available. The poor victim was given a stiff drink of rum and told to bite hard on a piece of cloth that one of the crew handed him. A couple of crewmen restrained the man and placed the mangled leg on the seat of a chair, and the carpenter began to saw. When he finished, the dismembered limb fell to the floor. To cauterize the new wound, the carpenter heated an axe until it was white hot and singed it against the bleeding stump.

Fern, who had been the ship's carpenter from the beginning, was replaced by a man named Edward Cheeseman. Cheeseman had been carpenter on the *Dolphin,* a ship that Phillips captured up on the Newfoundland Banks before sailing down to the West Indies, and although he had no interest in becoming a pirate, he was impressed into service because of his trade.

Following the trial and conviction of Thomas Fern, Phillips continued the voyage north, plundering over a dozen ships along the way until he reached the Banks of Newfoundland in April 1724. Searching around for a prize, Phillips fell in with a beautiful new fishing vessel, the *Squirrel.* It was so new that carpenters were still working to complete the finishing touches on the deck. It was owned and commanded by Captain Andrew Haradan, out of Annisquam, Massachusetts. Phillips liked the new vessel so much that he decided to make it his flagship. He had all his supplies, equipment and crew transferred over to the *Squirrel,* and after making himself and his crew "at home" on his new acquisition, he let all of the *Squirrel* crew except Captain Haradan go aboard the *Revenge* and sail off for home. Probably because of his seamanship as a skipper, Haradan was forcibly detained aboard his own ship.

Edward Cheeseman, the ship's new carpenter, had started conspiring against Phillips from the first. With Captain Haradan aboard, Cheeseman saw his chance to overthrow the pirate captain. He approached Haradan and within three days the two men initiated a mutiny. Most of the impressed men were eager to participate and they quickly formed a plan. Carpentry tools, which were still strewn around the unfinished deck, would be used as weapons. The overthrow was scheduled for noon, when the attackers would be able to clearly see what they were doing—and when their victims would least suspect a violent act.

At high noon on the chosen day, the mutineers were busy working on the deck. They moved about with hammers, knives and chisels. Heavier tools, like broadaxes and mallets, lay within reach. John Fillmore casually took a broadaxe in hand, and watched Cheeseman engage John Nutt in light conversation about the weather and other matters of concern to seamen. As Cheeseman and Nutt chatted away, Fillmore strolled over and started talking to the boatswain, the axe hanging loosely by his side as if he would be needing it in a few minutes to continue his work. The boatswain was turned away from John Nutt; he therefore didn't see Cheeseman's sudden attack. With a backward thrust, Cheeseman grabbed Nutt between the legs with one hand, and the back of his neck with the other. The startled pirate grabbed for the object that was shooting sharp pain through his genitals, only to find himself tipping backwards. In a split second, John Nutt was drowning in the freezing northern Atlantic. At almost the same instant, Fillmore, who was watching Cheeseman out of the corner of an eye, swiftly raised the broadaxe and brought it down onto the centre of the boatswain's skull, slicing it wide open like a codfish under a fish splitter's knife. During the fracas, other conspirators knocked unconscious the gunner, James Sparks, and another founding member of the piratical crew, and all were thrown overboard.

Phillips, who had been down in his cabin, finally heard the noise above and rushed up the ladder to the deck. As he emerged from below, Cheeseman swung a tremendous blow with a mallet, smashing Phillips's jaw to smithereens. Still conscious despite the blow to his face, Phillips charged Cheeseman—but before he reached him, Haradan intervened. He swung a broadaxe with all his might and hit Phillips on the head, knocking him dead with that one vicious blow. Cheeseman, seeing his opponent dead at the head of the ladder, went immediately below and herded up the remainder of the pirate crew.

With all Phillips's loyal men on deck, the victors behaved as badly as any voluntary band of pirates. They butchered ten of Phillips's men and threw them overboard. Dubious of the piratical status of the remainder, not knowing if they had been impressed, they locked them up to stand trial.

So Captain Haradan was again in command of his ship, and while he struck a course for his New England home, the new non-piratical crew sliced the head from Phillips's dead body and attached it to the ship's main mast. Then they threw the remains overboard.

Back in his home port, Haradan had the imprisoned men on board his ship sent ashore to stand trial. The majority—with the exception of John Rose Archer, whose record was badly blemished from serving under Blackbeard—were acquitted or reprieved.

Edward Low,

the Most Fiendish of All

One man's journey from devoted husband to tyrannical villian.

August 12, 1714, was a happy day for Eliza Marble: she was marrying Edward Low, a newcomer to Boston, New England. Eliza and Edward were very much in love, and their relatives and friends wished them well after a ceremony splendidly officiated by the Reverend Benjamin Wadsworth of Boston, who one day would become President of Harvard college.

Eliza may not have known much about Edward Low's family history. She may not have known that her new husband's older brother had been a highway man hanged at Tyburn, England. And certainly Eliza could not have surmised on this special day that her bridegroom would go down in history as one of the most fiendish and wicked pirates of all time; nor that in a few short years she would be dead.

Low was born in the parish of Westminster, England, and went to sea at an early age. Then one day on a shore visit at Boston, he met Eliza and she changed his life, at least for a time. He proposed marriage, Eliza accepted, and he signed off his ship and found work in a shipyard.

Low appears to have embraced an honest life in the outset. He held down his job at the shipyard and supported his wife, and for a time their marriage lived up to the promise of their wedding day. But life dealt some vicious blows. Low's first child died soon after birth, and Eliza died on the arrival of the second.

These losses seem to have impacted heavily on Low's disposition. He quarrelled with his co-workers and superiors at the shipyard and was subsequently fired.

Upon his dismissal from the shipyard, Low chose to return to a life at sea and signed onto a sloop bound for Honduras.

It may not have been known to Low and the other new recruits that the owner, captain, and mate of this ship were thieves; then again, even if they had known, it may not have mattered to them.

When the sloop reached Honduras, Low and twelve others were told to go ashore in a boat and steal logs of wood from the Spanish. As this work progressed, Low became the dominant person of the log-boat's crew. He must have possessed the quality of leadership that appeals to the wayward and unruly, the less-than-scrupulous, and the easily-influenced; he was admired by his workmates. Tough and mean, he was not to be trifled with—one can picture any member of the log-stealing crew who challenged Low's dominance suffering the penalty of a broken nose or busted jaw. Above all, Low undoubtedly projected an aura of authority. In his previous experience at sea, he had observed the ways of tough leadership, and now had the opportunity to put them to practice.

One day the captain ordered the men to make an extra trip to shore before dinner. Low and his men were hot, tired, and hungry. For Low the order was the straw that broke the camel's back. He threw a tantrum, raised his musket and shot the captain. Then Low and the other twelve men jumped back on board the log-stealing boat and rowed ashore. There on the beach Low told the men that he would be the captain of the log boat and that they would all follow his orders. He promised that they would be successful buccaneers, that they would become rich and live in luxury ashore. They would have loads of money to spend on rum, whores, fancy clothes, guns, knives, and anything else their thieving hearts desired. Low undoubtedly rationalized the situation—they had been stealing from the Spanish with no compensation for their dishonesty; they received no additional money above their meagre wages. So why not steal on their own and reap their just rewards?

A rough Jolly Roger was fashioned from scraps of cast-off clothing and strung on the main mast of the small log boat. This marked the beginning of Low's piratical career.

The following day found Low and his recruits at sea. Before long they fell in with a ship whose crew put up little resistance to their attackers; the vessel was easily captured, and Low was now certain he was ready for adventure on the high seas. There was a pirate rendezvous near Jamaica in the Grand Cayman Islands, and it was to this place that Low set sail in his newly captured prize.

The voyage went off without a hitch, and on reaching the Caymans, Low and his crew spent a few days outfitting their ship for bigger conquests. Here Low crossed paths with a well-known pirate, George Lowther. Low was impressed with Lowther's reputation and agreed to join forces: he would be Lowther's first lieutenant.

Lowther considered the ship Low had captured of little value and had it sunk. Low and his men boarded Lowther's larger vessel, the *Happy Delivery*, and struck out on a voyage of plunder and pillage.

On January 10, 1722, Captain Benjamin Edwards was sailing the Boston-owned *Greyhound* homeward when he was overtaken by Lowther and his pirate crew. Although Captain Edwards put up a hard battle of resistance for more than two hours, exchanging cannon balls, one for one, in the end he was no match for Lowther and his cutthroats. Realizing that he would not be able to stop the vicious onslaught, Edwards surrendered, thinking this would at least end the violence. But when Lowther and his men boarded the *Greyhound*, they were sorely disappointed. All that fighting, all those cannonballs—and this ship carried merely a load of wood! Furious, Lowther and his crew took out their anger and disappointment on the captured crew. Two sailors were suspended from the mainmast and viciously whipped, and then the *Greyhound* was set afire. Captain Edwards and his crew were taken aboard the *Happy Delivery*, where seven men were impressed.

The conquests continued, with seven vessels out of Boston alone succumbing to Lowther's force, and soon Low once again became a pirate captain. Lowther's fleet fell upon a sleek and handsome sloop out of Newport, and Low was appointed her commander. Then a fine Jamaican sloop was seized and Charles Harris, an impressed sailor from the *Greyhound* who showed considerable piratical promise as a competent mariner and leader, was given command. Lowther's fleet now consisted of three fine ships, a small sloop for a tender, and one hundred sea marauders.

Having assembled this small but well-commanded and well-equipped pirate fleet, Lowther was ready to prey on more lustrous game—but first the ships needed considerable maintenance work. Their hulls were heavily coated with barnacles and badly in need of scraping. Port Mayo at Matique had good careening grounds, so the pirate fleet sailed there before setting out on another voyage of plunder.

The scraping and cleaning would be time consuming, taking up a week or more, so the pirates set up a small colony on the shore and stored their plunder in tents pitched on the beach, near the water.

The work progressed well, until one day, while they were attending to the hull of the *Happy Delivery*, a band of natives let out blood-curdling screams and charged out of the jungle that bordered the beach. Unprepared for this attack, the pirates dropped their tools and sprinted for their little tenders pulled up at the water's edge. Pushing off and away from the shore, the pirates escaped their attackers and took refuge in the sloops that were anchored nearby.

The natives ransacked the tents on the beach and ran off with food supplies and precious plunder. The pirates were furious. They cursed and fought and swore, blaming each other for being unprepared for such an attack and not fighting off the enemy. It was only with considerable persuasion that Lowther and Low managed to settle down their thieving crew.

As the natives swarmed over the careened *Happy Delivery*, taking everything they could, Lowther decided that the treasure was not worth the potential loss of his men in a fight with the natives. The vessel was plundered even of its canvas and rope rigging, quickly becoming useless.

Lowther had earlier taken as his own ship another vessel, larger than the *Happy Delivery*. His new acquisition, renamed the *Ranger,* was spacious and sturdy and built for warfare. It had five cannons on both the port and starboard sides, eight of which could be swivelled for accurate shots. Lowther reasoned that a well-armed and adequately manned vessel would be more effective in an engagement than his well-armed, poorly manned craft accompanied by two shabby sloops. With this in mind, Lowther decided to consolidate all the fleet's resources aboard his newest vessel. He had Edward Low and Charles Harris sink their sloops and board the *Ranger* with their crews and all their stores. Lowther and some one hundred sea marauders then hauled anchor and set sail in search of floating fortunes.

It was inevitable that Edward Low and Captain George Lowther would one day part company. Low was belligerent and quarrelsome; he had a cruel side to his nature that matched or surpassed that of Captain Lowther; and he was ambitious. Lowther had made a mistake in letting Low join his fleet. Low was a pirate captain of his own ship and commanded his own crew of pirates when he met Lowther, and Lowther should have expected the marauders under Low's control to retain their loyalty to Low. The piratical leadership that had initially won over the crew of the log boat did not diminish when Low became Lowther's lieutenant. Indeed, Lowther even gave Low a golden opportunity to befriend and win over members of Lowther's own crew when he brought Low and his men aboard the *Happy Delivery*.

Several weeks went by after the crews consolidated without another vessel passing. As days turned to weeks, the pirates grew restless and morale ran low. This was a perfect time for Low to listen to the gripes of the unhappy buccaneers, sympathize with them, and further build his image as the best man to lead the fleet.

Mutiny might have broken out under Low's direction if the crew hadn't finally taken a small brigantine, several weeks after leaving the beached *Happy Delivery*. It was a minor conquest, but it elevated the pirates' spirits. Morale was further raised a short time later when, while sailing for the Bahamas, Lowther captured the brigantine *Rebecca* which was on a course for Boston.

Now, Lowther may have decided to make a move before he lost all control to his ambitious lieutenant. He turned the *Rebecca* over to Low and bade him farewell. It was the afternoon of May 28, 1722 and Lowther obviously made the right decision. Almost half of Lowther's crew joined Low.

Lowther happily watched Low sail away that day in May. He watched the departure of a man who would go down in history as the most cruel and brutal pirate to sail the North Atlantic.

On splitting off with Captain Lowther, Low set a course for the coasts of New England and Nova Scotia with some forty cutthroat pirates aboard. A couple of weeks later, Low reached the coast of New England and plundered a sloop out of New Jersey. On that same day he fell in with another sloop, this one from Newport. It is unclear what exactly occurred in this engagement, but the captain, James Cahoon, escaped: news of Low's attack on Captain Cahoon's sloop reached Newport Harbour the following morning.

Low apparently expected trouble when Cahoon escaped—he fled the scene of the attack. It was a wise move. The day Newport Harbour received the news of piratical activity, two ships sailed to capture Low and his sea brigands. One was equipped with ten guns and carried eighty men; the other had six guns and sixty men. But Low was lucky! A wind sprang up in his favour and he escaped his pursuers.

News that Low was in the region soon reached Boston. Over a hundred volunteers were rounded up to catch the sea rovers. The men thought they had succeeded in hunting the culprit down when a ship on the horizon was identified as the *Rebecca*. But when it was overtaken, the disappointed group found only a crew on a homeward journey to Marblehead. Guessing that others would be out to try and track him down, the cunning Low had abandoned the *Rebecca* and transferred to another ship.

The sea posse returned home with the *Rebecca* and the volunteers from Boston stopped searching for Low. Meanwhile, Low and his sea dogs were in Buzzard Bay, not far from Newport, stealing sheep for food from isolated pastures and taking on fresh water.

At this point, Low could have chosen to sail back to the Caribbean, but instead decided to set a course for the eastern end of Nova Scotia, which runs far out into the Atlantic. It was sufficiently distant from the New England coast to offer safety from Newport and Boston law enforcers. Also, there was real potential for easy plunder in the more northern region, primarily populated by the French. Furthermore, Low's New England enemy may well have presumed that he was by now far on his way back to southern waters; similarly, the French and British of Nova Scotia would probably not guess he had fled to their region.

Low reached Roseway Harbour, near Shelburne, Nova

Scotia, a couple of weeks after his escape from the New Englanders. He and his marauders approached the small harbour with considerable stealth, skilfully hiding their presence in the area.

There, a fleet of thirteen fishing vessels lay anchored. This was a terrific find and Low devised a way to take them all without hassle: Under the cover of darkness, a fishing vessel would be approached by a small boat. One of Low's crew would call out, "Permission to come aboard," and they were always welcomed. It was common for visitors to drop by, looking to borrow or trade something or just to chat and socialize. Once on board, the pirates drew pistols and cutlasses hidden in their clothing. The defenseless fishermen were then held captive and their ships plundered. In this fashion Low systematically pillaged all thirteen vessels, taking everything of value.

After all the schooners had been stripped of food supplies and useful materials, Low impressed about a dozen of the fishermen and allowed the rest to go free.

One of the impressed fishermen was a young Marblehead lad, Philip Ashton, to be known as the "Marblehead Robinson Crusoe." Ashton refused to join the pirates and to sign articles, and was subsequently whipped and threatened with death. In March 1723, he escaped on the island of Roatan, in the Bay of Honduras, where he survived on crabs, fish, bird eggs, and the like for sixteen months until he was rescued by a ship from Salem, Massachusetts.

Low took a fancy to a fine Marblehead schooner of the fishing fleet, the *Mary*, and he chose it as a replacement for the *Rebecca*, abandoned to evade his Boston pursuers. All crewmembers, stores, and valuables were transferred to the *Mary*, and the Marblehead fishermen were allowed to return home on the ship Low had been sailing since he left the *Rebecca*. Low then named his new flagship *Fancy*.

Departing Roseway in his new acquisition, the *Fancy*, Low continued on up the coast to Newfoundland where he tried to capture a large ship in St. John's Harbour. The prey turned out to be a heavily armed man-of-war, and Low quickly aborted the attack and raced back out to sea. Sailing further to the north along the Newfoundland coast, Low entered Conception Bay and terrorized and pillaged a small village near Carbonear. Following that felonious caper, Low attacked and plundered eight fishing vessels—some Portuguese and French—on the Newfoundland Grand Banks.

With a hold full of dried and salted cod fish and other pilfered food supplies, Low headed back down towards southern waters and, along the way, ran into a ferocious hurricane. The storm wreaked havoc at Port-Royal in the south, destroying forty vessels and killing about four hundred people, but Low and his men were either skilful or lucky; the *Fancy* survived the storm relatively unscathed.

After the storm subsided, Low fell in with a large ship that was severely crippled by the hurricane. It had lost its masts and was floating at the whim of the tides and currents. The old saying, "one man's loss is another man's gain," was applicable, as Low plundered the great ship and was delighted with a "cold cash" heist of about a thousand pounds in gold and silver. Low may have impressed some of the captured crew, and it is likely that those who didn't join the ranks of his sea brigands were left aboard the crippled ship, once again at the mercy of the unforgiving sea.

Low headed back down the eastern coast, capturing several ships along the way. Again he chose a bigger and stauncher vessel to be his flagship. This time it was a former British man-of-war, the *Rose*, which he took with little resistance. The *Fancy* was then placed in the charge of Charles Harris, who had chosen to leave Lowther and be led by Low.

Shortly after the *Rose* was taken, Harris captured a galley and allowed his crew to prowl around its decks, slashing and slicing the prisoners with their cutlasses. Low was on board at the time, enjoying the excitement of the slaughter, when one of the pirates accidentally sliced him across the lower jaw, baring his bottom teeth. The fleet surgeon stitched up the wound, but not to Low's satisfaction. Low went into a rage and cursed and swore all manner of insults at the surgeon. The surgeon lost his temper, laid back and threw a hard punch at Low's mangled jaw. "Sew it up your self!" he howled. The surgeon's services were so badly needed by the fleet that Low calmed down and let the incident rest without further comment.

Low hated the Portuguese, and two Roman Catholic friars of that nationality were aboard. He and Harris had them hung from a mast by ropes tied to their wrists. When the unfortunate men passed out from pain and fatigue, they were lowered to the deck and revived. Then they were again hoisted aloft and left hanging until they passed out. This procedure was repeated over and over until both died, at which point they were tossed overboard to the sharks.

Following this murderous day, Low struck a course for the port of Madeira, Spain, stopped there for a short time, and then sailed down to Western Africa and captured the *Liverpool Merchant* and the *King Sagamore* off the Cape Verde Islands.

After going ashore and careening his ships, Low set sail for the coast of Brazil, but, never encountering a ship there worth capturing, moved northward.

One day on the northward voyage, after plundering and seizing several vessels, Low encountered an extremely rich prize, the galleon *Nostra Signiora de Victoria* of Portugal. Some of the Portuguese sailors were interrogated about the location of the ship's treasure, even though this information was probably kept a secret from the crew. Low had the sailors tortured, so in desperation they likely made up a story. They told Low that the captain placed the total fortune worth about fifty thousand dollars in a heavy woven cloth bag and hung it out of his cabin window on a rope. They said that when the captain saw that Low's pirates were winning the battle and the *Nostra Signiora* was about to be seized, he cut the rope and the treasure dropped into the sea. It was an unlikely story, but Low bought it.

In an uncontrollable rage, Low had the captain tied to a mast, then drew his cutlass and slashed off the poor man's lips and nose. He then had the cook broil the dismembered flesh and forced the captain's mate to eat it. Having worked himself into a wild frenzy by his depraved acts, he had the entire crew of the *Nostra Signiora de Victoria* slaughtered in cold blood.

Low's murderous conduct displayed in the *Nostra Signiora de Victoria* fracas was not unprecedented. He disliked the men of New England—perhaps because of his dismissal from the Boston shipyard, the siege against his fleet, or the fact that Boston was a port where many pirates were hanged. But that dislike was far surpassed by his hatred of the Spanish. When he captured a Spanish vessel that had earlier taken several New England ships, he ordered his cutthroats to murder the entire Spanish crew. His pirates went about the decks of the captured ship, chopping and slicing the crew to pieces with poleaxes and cutlasses. Some of the Spanish men jumped overboard only to be shot as they splashed around in the water. Several badly wounded victims managed to swim ashore. A few days later some of Low's pirates were strolling along the shore when one of the wounded survivors struggled out of the undergrowth along the edge of the beach and begged for mercy and lodging on Low's ship. One of the pirates responded by shoving the end of his musket down the poor wretch's throat and blasting out his innards.

Shortly following the capture of the *Nostra Signiora de Victoria*, Low continued on his northerly voyage. All went well until June 1723, when he reached a point near New York and news of his presence hit town. A man-of-war quickly set sail to capture the pilfering pirate. Low was sighted early one morning and a ferocious battle ensued, during which he struggled to out-run his pursuers. The man-of-war was gaining on Low until the wind suddenly died down. Low got the ship tender boats afloat and gained distance by rowing his vessels away from the much heavier man-of-war. Eventually, after a lot of hard rowing, Low managed to escape. Charles Harris was less fortunate: he, his crew, and his schooner were all captured.

Continuing northerly, Low fell in with a whaler about eighty miles off Nantucket Island. Boarding the vessel, Low ordered his men to strip the captain naked, slice his ears off, and shoot him through the head. On completing this sadistic act, Low sunk the ship. Some of the whalers managed to escape Low's pirates by rowing away in a small boat to another vessel in the area, and thus the story of Low's diabolical act became well known to New England residents.

A couple of days later, Low went mad. He had the captain of a captured fishing vessel dragged aboard and held while he slashed away at him with his cutlass. Finally, when there was little left to maim, he decapitated him in one fell swoop of the cutlass. On the same day, the master of another vessel was hauled aboard. Low cut a hole in the man's chest, pulled out his heart, and roasted it on a grill. Repeating the heinous act of the *Nostra Signioria de Victoria*, Low forced the captain's mate to eat the heart. Shortly afterward, Low had the captain of still another captured vessel hauled on board. Low sliced off the poor unfortunate's ears and roasted them over a fire. Then he cut the flesh into small pieces, sprinkled it with salt and pepper, and "gave" it to that captain's crew for lunch.

It is difficult to trace the rest of Low's movements, but it's probable that in the late summer or fall of 1723 he entered the Bay of Fundy and sailed up the Nova Scotia coast. Low's ships were probably again in need of maintenance and the Bay offers the best careening grounds in the world—tides in the Minas Basin rise as high as fifty feet or more. What better place could a pirate ask for than the Bay of Fundy to work on the hull of a ship? In the upper reaches of the Bay a ship could remain high and dry for almost twelve hours.

Now, although Low's reason for visiting the Bay of Fundy was probably to careen the ships, a treasure map acquired in 1947 by historian and author Edward Rowe Snow indicates that Low visited Isle Haute, in the Bay of Fundy, and buried a treasure from the *Nostra Signiora de Victoria*—Low had apparently located the treasure over which he slaughtered the Portuguese captain. The treasure map lists the loot in Low's ship as 23,758 pieces of eight and 1,335 pieces of gold.

As time went by, Low's diabolical behaviour worsened and his sadistic capers increased. His methods of torture and murder varied—sometimes he simply hanged his victims, while at other times he was gruesomely inventive. A time came when even his depraved followers could not put up with his demented ways.

The details of the incident are unknown, but eventually Edward Low was abandoned by his own men. In the spring of 1724, a French warship that had been dispatched to hunt Low down found him adrift in an open boat with three of his men. He had infuriated his crew by murdering his quartermaster. His men could take no more. They had mutinied and cast him and three other intolerable pirates adrift without food or water.

Low and the three castaways were taken to Martinique where they were tried by the French court for piracy and hanged.

Edward and Margaret Jordan,
the Pirate Couple

Mutiny and treachery off the coast of Nova Scotia.

Captain John Stairs caught a glimpse of a shiny object in his peripheral vision as he leaned over the chart table down in the ship's cabin. Turning towards the skylight above his head, he was startled to see the barrel of a pistol from outside pressed against the windowpane. Then there was a flash of fire as if a candle had been lit and instantly muffed out. The skylight shattered, accompanied by a deafening blast like a clap of lightening. Surprise came before pain. A bullet had sliced a shallow groove across the side of his nose and face but he only became aware that he had been shot when a spurt of blood splattered off the clean chart on the table below his chin.

Captain Stairs was not alone. Thomas Heath, seaman and pilot, who had been standing by his side, keeled over and fell to his knees on the floor. He had taken the slug directly in the chest—it had barely missed punching a hole through Stair's head.

As soon as Captain Stairs recovered from the fright and the initial sting of gun powder lodged in his face, he lunged to his trunk for his pistols but found them missing. The trunk had been forced open. He then searched for his cutlass, but it was nowhere to be found.

Unarmed, Stairs leapt up the ladder from the cabin to the deck. At the top, before him, was passenger Edward Jordan, a pistol in one hand and an axe in the other, about to descend.

Captain Stairs lunged and clutched Jordan by both arms. As Jordan fought to free himself, he cocked his pistol to fire. Stairs grabbed the gun by the muzzle, gave it a violent twist, and, before Jordan could pull the trigger, wrenched it free. Throwing the pistol overboard, Stairs concentrated on the axe swinging back and forth towards his head. As he fought to wrench the murderous axe from Jordan's grip, he screamed for his mate, John Kelly, to help him. But Kelly had teamed up with Jordan to take over the ship, and didn't answer. The two men wrestled for the axe, falling down and rolling on the deck. Stairs managed to wrench the axe free of Jordan's grip, and slung it overboard.

Again Stairs called for Kelly, and this time saw him standing nearby with his back towards Stairs. He was loading a pistol.

As Stairs and Jordan rolled and wrestled on the deck, Stairs was attacked from above by a second person: Jordan's wife, Margaret. She had grabbed the nearest weapon in sight, a boat hook. Over and over she struck Stairs with the boat hook handle as he fought to subdue his assailant.

Meanwhile, Thomas Heath had managed to crawl on deck and lay dead in a pool of blood on the starboard side of the vessel.

Crew member Benjamin Matthews, who appeared to be wounded, came running to help. But when he reached the site of combat he found himself being attacked by Jordan, who had freed himself from Stairs and now wielded another axe. Jordan knocked Matthews to the deck, striking him several times on the back of the head until he killed him.

Realizing he was no match for the two armed fanatics and desperate to escape Jordan's murderous axe, Stairs, with incredible strength, hauled a hatch cover over to the side of the ship, flung it overboard and jumped in after it.

As Captain Stairs clung to the floating hatch cover, Jordan and Kelly appeared at the side of the vessel. Jordan was now holding another pistol, and aimed it at Stairs, who bobbed up and down with the waves. "Don't waste your ammunition trying to hit him," Kelly told Jordan. "He's done for. He'll drown in a few hours. It's too far to swim to shore." Jordan uncocked the pistol and watched Captain Stairs float away to perish from hypothermia in the cold salt water.

The year was 1809. On or about July 17, Captain John Stairs of the fishing schooner *Three Sisters*, owned by Jonathan and John Tremain, sailed out of Halifax, Nova Scotia, for Perce, Quebec, on the east coast of the Gaspé Peninsula. His crew consisted of his mate, John Kelly, and two mariners, Thomas Heath, seaman and pilot and Benjamin Matthews, seaman.

The schooner carried two passengers: a black-bearded Irishman, Edward Jordan, and another man named Patrick Cinnet. Jordan was on his way home to Perce, where he had arranged to have the *Three Sisters* loaded with a cargo of fish for shipment to Halifax.

The *Three Sisters* reached its destination around the first of August. In early September, the schooner took on about six hundred quintals (a quintal is equal to a hundred pounds) of fish. On September 10, Captain Stairs pulled anchor and headed back for Halifax. Along with him and his tiny crew—consisting of John Kelly, Thomas Heath and Benjamin Matthews—were Edward Jordan, his wife, Margaret, and their four children, three girls and a boy.

The cruise went along smoothly until September 13. That was the fateful day Edward Jordan, Margaret Jordan, and Captain Stairs's mate, John Kelly, showed their piratical colours, and Captain Stairs said goodbye to the *Three Sisters* as he bobbed up and down, holding fast to a ship's hatch cover.

This brutal piratical incident took place between Cape Canso and Whitehead Island, in the Atlantic Ocean, off the easternmost tip of mainland Nova Scotia.

As Captain Stairs drifted away from his schooner, Edward Jordan took command. Throwing the two dead bodies overboard, he set a course north-easterly towards Cape Breton Island.

Meanwhile, Captain Stairs hung to his little hatch cover raft. Drowning was probably less painful than being axed to death, but that was all Stairs had as a consolation. Still, his survival instinct was robust, and rather than surrendering to the depths of the sea, he hung on and on to his hatch cover....

Hours went by. Stairs knew that it would not be long before he lost consciousness in the freezing water. Thoughts of the murderous fracas haunted his mind, though, and he could not stop repeating the day's events in his mind: It was a bright, sunny morning. Thomas Heath had followed him below deck; Stairs had gone below to get his quadrant to take a sun shot. *Why had he been unarmed when he encountered Jordan?* Memories returned. When the shot was fired and Heath fell to the floor, Stairs had immediately lunged for the pistols in his trunk—but none were there. The trunk had been unlocked. His pistols were missing and so was his cutlass. Who had taken them? Kelly? Jordan? Margaret Jordan?

After hours in the freezing water, kept afloat only by the hatch cover, Stairs probably didn't see the sail appear on the horizon. It belonged to an American schooner en route for Hingham, Massachusetts. One of the schooner's crew spotted the body of a man clutching a ship's hatch cover, sloshing up and down in the waves.

Captain Stairs was taken aboard. He thanked God for his good fortune and the American captain and crew. He also requested to be landed at Halifax, but the captain refused because he was afraid of having his men impressed. On his outward bound voyage, his pilot had been taken by the *Bream* or *Mullet* Schooner. Stairs then asked to be put off before passing Cape Sable, but wind conditions didn't oblige, and he stayed on board until the ship reached its destination: Hingham, Massachusetts.

Captain Stairs most gratefully thanked the Yankee captain and the crew and went directly to Boston where he met with the British consul and told his story. The consul sent letters to major ports along the eastern Atlantic Coast to watch for the *Three Sisters* and its pirate crew.

Back on the stolen schooner, Edward Jordan and his tiny but loathsome pirate crew sailed up the south-eastern coast of Cape Breton Island, crossed the Cabot Strait and put into Fortune Bay, on the southern cost of Newfoundland.

Jordan and his pirate mates spent a few days in a small inlet of Fortune Bay and impressed an unwilling seaman, John Pigot. Then, Jordan sailed back out to sea and easterly to the Avalon Peninsula and anchored at St. Mary's. After several days, Jordan pulled anchor and set off up the coast in search of a navigator to guide them across to Ireland.

After visiting a couple of ports and making inquiries, Jordan found a navigator named Patrick Power who agreed to do the job. A monthly wage was established and an agreement signed.

Just before they were about to leave, trouble broke out between John Kelly and Jordan. Kelly had apparently been a little too friendly with Margaret Jordan, and the two men fell into a fight. Kelly drew his pistol and the navigator, Patrick Power, disarmed him. A few days later, Kelly apparently decided he'd feel safer away from Jordan: he jumped into a small boat, rowed away, and was never seen or heard from again.

As soon as Kelly was gone, tempers calmed down, and Jordan, with a half-dozen new crewmen aboard, weighed anchor with the intention of beginning the Atlantic crossing over to Ireland. As he headed out to sea, it appeared that he was being followed or pursued. He became quite apprehensive and continually asked the members of his crew what they thought was going on. It soon became evident that he was in deep trouble when the ship, growing larger and larger as it caught up, was identified as a King's schooner. It was His Majesty's Schooner *Cuttle*, sent out to hunt Jordan by order of the British consul's office in Boston.

The *Cuttle* signalled that it was sending a boarding party over to the *Three Sisters*. Jordan, in a panic, instructed navigator Patrick Power to say they were en route to Halifax, Nova Scotia, but the lie failed. The leader of the boarding party announced that Captain Stairs was alive and had reported the piracy. Jordan and the crew were placed under arrest and the *Three Sisters* was escorted to Halifax where the pirates were thrown into jail to await trial and conviction.

After the trial proceedings, it took less than an hour for the court to reach an unanimous accord. Edward Jordan was found guilty of murder, piracy and robbery and sentenced to be hanged.

Margaret Jordan was extremely lucky. The court had trouble ascertaining her part in the crime, and she was the mother of four children who would become orphans should she be executed. Margaret was pronounced "not guilty" and set free.

Edward Jordan was hanged on November 23, 1809 near the foot of present-day Inglis Street, in Halifax. His tarred and chained corpse was hung on a gibbet at the entrance to Halifax Harbour as a warning to others of the severity of punishment for piracy.

𝕭lackbeard,
the East Coast Menace

The story of the pirate with hellfire in his eyes, and how he came to our doorstep.

Edward Teach was one of the most ferocious and feared pirates to pilfer and plunder along the Atlantic East Coast. Better known as Blackbeard, Teach preyed on all shipping up and down the North American eastern shore. With a band of cutthroat buccaneers, he invaded fishing villages, stealing everything of value and molesting women of all ages.

Teach earned the name "Blackbeard" for his fearsome appearance. He wore a jet-black beard that almost covered his entire face. Only his eyes, the tip of his sunburnt nose, and chapped lips were visible. He made good use of this awesome appearance: one look at the face full of black hair was enough to unnerve the most worthy adversary. Honest, God-fearing men, not used to fighting others to survive, were intimidated by this awful man's appearance that was more canine than human. Women fainted and children screamed in horror at the sight of him. His beard was long and he braided it into pigtails, tied the ends with ribbons, and tucked them back up over his ears. He made the most of his frightening appearance in battle to scare his opponents.

Three braces of pistols hung in holsters from his shoulders. He made his eyes look wild and supernatural by reflecting light off them from fire that burned from the ends of hemp tucked under his hat. Blackbeard was, indeed, a "piece of work," intended to overwhelm his foes by the appearance of a creature straight out of hell.

As well as paying special attention to his grooming, Blackbeard took particular care of his sexual needs. Acquiring one girl after another, he ended up with thirteen wives. It's unlikely that his unsavoury appearance held any attraction, so either they were willing to put up with anything for his money or—more probably—he used real or threatened force to get what he wanted. One version of his love-life tells of him falling in love with a fifteen-year-old girl who lived on a plantation in North Carolina. After the marriage ceremony, he went to her family's plantation for the honeymoon and brought along a bunch of his merry sea brigands. He and his buddies caroused, gambled, and drank rum night and day throughout the entire stay, utterly destroying the poor bride's expectations of a happy marriage.

Born in Bristol, England, Blackbeard went to sea at an early age, and somewhere along the way became a pirate. In 1716, Blackbeard served with the pirate crew of Benjamin Thornigold. The following year, Thornigold, with Blackbeard on board, was in the West Indies when he decided to sail to the east coast of North America. Setting a course from New Providence, Thornigold captured several ships along the way and let Blackbeard take command of one of the vessels. This marked the beginning of Blackbeard's individual marauding career. Thornigold decided to take advantage of the king's proclamation offering pardon to all pirates who would reform. He turned around and returned to New Providence where he turned himself in to the king's authorities, leaving Blackbeard to go as he wished.

Blackbeard named his ship *Queen Anne's Revenge*, mounted forty good-sized guns taken from recently captured vessels, and set out to make a fortune as a highwayman of the sea.

Out on the high seas, Blackbeard won fame as a bold and dangerous pirate. One of his first conquests was the pilfering of an excellent vessel, the *Great Allan*. After transferring all the *Great Allan's* valuables aboard the *Queen Anne's Revenge*, he put the captured crew ashore on an island and set the fine ship on fire.

Blackbeard furthered his notorious reputation when he was attacked by the British man-of-war *Scarborough*. He fought his adversaries so violently that, after several hours of horrendous bloodshed on both sides, the British crew gave up the fight and withdrew. The warship sailed away for cover in the nearest port. News of Blackbeard's triumph over the British man-of-war swept both sides of the Atlantic and placed him high on the list of notorious pirates.

One victory for Blackbeard is no less than humorous. He fell in with a handsome sloop named the *Revenge,* owned by a Major Stede Bonnet, a man one might call a "gentleman pirate." Bonnet was a man of good reputation who owned an estate on the island of Barbados. He had taken to the sea as a pirate just for the excitement and adventure of the game. In short, Bonnet had taken up piracy as a "hobby," something to add a little spice to his life. He knew nothing about the art of navigation, so Blackbeard offered to "help out." He befriended the major and arranged an exchange of sorts: Bonnet was appointed lieutenant on the *Queen Anne's Revenge,* and an experienced navigator from Blackbeard's crew went over to the *Revenge.* Blackbeard told Bonnet that since Bonnet had no experience that qualified him to be his lieutenant, he would not have to do any work or perform any duties. His life at sea would be one of leisure where he would follow his "own inclinations." With the exchange of places, Blackbeard sent one of his pirates, a man by the name of Richards, over to take command of the *Revenge*—and thus, without any bloodshed, Blackbeard took possession of the ship he had coveted.

Not long after taking Bonnet's ship, Blackbeard fell in with and captured a sloop taking on fresh water at Turneffe Island, in the Gulf of Honduras. The vessel was called the *Adventure*, commanded by a Captain David Harriot. Blackbeard transferred Harriot and his crew over to the *Queen Anne's Revenge*. Then, he moved some of his own crew to the *Adventure*, and placed one of his cronies, Israel Hands, in command. (In his book *Treasure Island*, Robert Louis Stevenson used the name "Israel Hands" for one of his pirates.)

By now Blackbeard's reputation was such that no one seemed to dare resist him. In early April 1717, he fell in with a large ship and four sloops while sailing in the Gulf of Honduras. The large ship was the *Protestant Caesar*, out of Boston. When Blackbeard hoisted the Jolly Roger and fired a shot across the bow of the ship, its captain and crew immediately abandoned the vessel and fled ashore in their rowboats. The ship and sloops were ransacked and the *Protestant Caesar* and one sloop were set afire.

Following the episode with the *Protestant Caesar* and sloops, Blackbeard began sailing for the eastern coast of North America, capturing and plundering several ships along the way. Upon reaching the shores of the North American mainland, Blackbeard worked his way up near the entrance of Charleston Harbour, South Carolina, and waited like a cat for a mouse: whenever a ship came out of the harbour, Blackbeard would take it. Over a period of several days, he captured five vessels, taking all crews captive on the *Queen Anne's Revenge*. News of Blackbeard's presence swept up and down the coast, paralyzing shipping in and out of Charleston Harbour and trapping eight vessels in the harbour. After robbing the prisoners of the five captured ships, taking about fifteen hundred pounds' worth of gold and silver, he let them go free and continued up the coast towards North Carolina with a fleet consisting of his flagship, the *Queen Anne's Revenge*, two other ships, and a small sloop that served as a tender.

Around this time, while sailing up the coast, Blackbeard decided to follow the course of action taken by his mentor, pirate Benjamin Thornigold, and take advantage of the king's proclamation offering piratical pardons. To this end he made a few alterations to improve his appearance before applying for clemency. He destroyed the *Queen Anne's Revenge* and the two ships by running them aground, piled all his men aboard the small sloop, purposely overloading it, and marooned many of the pirates (excluding his favourites) on an island a few miles off the mainland. Major Bonnet, who now had his own ship back, rescued the stranded men a few days later. Blackbeard distributed all the loot and money among his friends and, like any ordinary skipper of honest means, appeared before Governor Charles Eden and requested pardon.

Governor Eden saw in Blackbeard a chance to make a lot of money. Instead of processing the application for clemency, he had a court of Vice-Admiralty declare Blackbeard to be only a privateer, and an honest one. This miscarriage of justice enabled Blackbeard to lay claim to a Spanish ship that he had earlier captured, even though England and Spain had not been at war at the time. Governor Eden was amply rewarded, and future benefits to him were implied.

In the spring of 1718, Blackbeard sailed far up the east coast on a voyage of pillage and plunder. Shortly after robbing three English ships of food and supplies, he fell in with two rich French sloops. He captured both, put all the loot on his ship, let the French crews go free on one of the crafts, and returned to North Carolina, where he shared the spoils with Governor Eden. To prove that all was legal and above board, Blackbeard gave oath that the two French vessels had been adrift and badly in need of rescue. Eden convened a court which declared the French sloop condemned.

Not all prominent men shared Governor Eden's acceptance of the notorious Blackbeard; nor were they disposed to sharing the spoils of his exploits. Lieutenant Robert Maynard, commander of the British man-of-war *Pearl*, was one of Blackbeard's fiercest critics. He vowed to hunt down and kill this culprit who pillaged and plundered up and down the North American east coast. Accompanied by another man-of-war, the *Lime*, Maynard found Blackbeard near the mouth of the Ocracoke Inlet of Cape Hatteras, North Carolina.

Governor Eden's secretary, a Mr. Knight, who had also received some of Blackbeard's plunder, learned of Maynard's venture and quickly notified Blackbeard of the planned attack. Blackbeard was, therefore, not surprised when he saw two sails appear on the horizon. He prepared to do battle.

It was starting to get dark when Maynard sighted the spars and masts of Blackbeard's ship. Preferring to wage battle during the day, he dropped anchor for the night.

Early the following morning, Maynard hoisted the British flag and struck out to capture the notorious buccaneer. Almost within range to engage the pirate ship, the wind suddenly died down and both Maynard and Blackbeard were becalmed. Maynard waited for a while, but soon became anxious over the prospect of the wind returning in Blackbeard's favour. He ordered his men to row the *Pearl* and the *Lime* over to within boarding reach of the pirate ship. Working feverishly at the oars, Maynard's men forced the vessels to gain on the becalmed pirates. Just when it appeared that they were in a winning position, Blackbeard let go with a ferocious volley of cannon fire. Maynard's vessels were without cannon and unable to retaliate. The destruction was horrendous. About thirty of Maynard's men were killed or wounded and one of the vessels was temporarily disabled. But Maynard was determined to win. He sent all his men but the helmsman below deck and waited. The wind came up briefly, and Maynard's ship scraped up against the pirate vessel. From that point on, all hell broke loose.

Blackbeard and his cutthroats jumped over onto the deck of Maynard's craft, thinking that there was no opposition. But at the same moment, Maynard's men emerged from below. Pistols fired, cutlass clashed against cutlass, and men on both sides fell dead or wounded.

While the battle raged on, Maynard recognized Blackbeard and opened fire on him with his pistol, wounding but not killing him. Blackbeard immediately fired back and missed. Blackbeard lunged and took a ferocious swing of his cutlass that snapped Maynard's sword off at the handle. Then he took another swing at Maynard that probably would have decapitated him had it not been for one of the British marines. The marine deflected the stroke and landed a dreadful blow to Blackbeard's neck—but the fight was still not over. Blackbeard put up a long and hard fight against his assailants, suffering some twenty sword blows and five pistol wounds. Then he began to lose his strength. From the loss of blood and fatigue, he wavered. He tried to cock his pistol to fire another shot, but instead slumped forward and fell dead on the deck.

After the dead bodies were rounded up and the wounded taken below, Blackbeard's head was severed from his body and hung from the bowsprit of Maynard's victorious man-of-war.

Searching the pirate ship, Lieutenant Maynard found some letters addressed to Edward Teach, a.k.a. Blackbeard, from prominent residents of the North Atlantic east coast. Some were extremely incriminating, the foremost being from Secretary Knight of North Carolina. One of those letters mentioned twenty barrels of sugar given by Teach to Secretary Knight and sixty to Governor Charles Eden of North Carolina.

William Kidd,
the Nova Scotia Treasure Icon

The story behind the most famous pirate of all.

N o pirate has permeated present-day consciousness like Captain William Kidd. But Kidd is not infamous, like Blackbeard, for his tyranny or cruelty. His legacy appeals to one of our most base instincts: greed. People have been searching the booby-trapped Oak Island for two hundred years, convinced that Kidd is behind the elaborate engineering there—despite extensive evidence to the contrary. (See my 1993 book *Oak Island Gold* for more on this story.)

So why William Kidd? Why has his name become synonymous with treasure? Much of the reason lies in folklore and legend passed down through generations—stories of ancestors who helped to bury booty, of treasure maps, of Kidd's enormous wealth. There is hardly a beach, harbour, or island from Newfoundland to Florida that hasn't been the reputed burial cache of Captain Kidd's riches.

Still, few know of Kidd beyond his association with treasure. His life story, complete with mutiny, treachery, and, of course, danger, is fascinating. Historians still study the details of his time as a captain of the high seas, and astonishingly enough, many agree that this most famous of pirates was not a pirate at all.

Details of Kidd's childhood and youth are obscure, but he is believed to have been born in Greenock, Scotland. The year of his birth is pure guesswork. In 1701 a Newgate prison chaplain, Paul Lorraine, placed him at "about 56 years of age." Assuming the estimate was close, Kidd was born around 1645.

Kidd spent most of his life at sea, beginning in his boyhood. He was pressed into the navy in 1673 and was a crew member of the *Prince Royal* during the Dutch wars.

By 1680 he had resigned from the navy and bought his own ship. Eight years later he settled in New York, bought a house, and began courting Mrs. Sarah Oort, the wife of a shipmaster-merchant. Illiterate but lovely and accomplished, Sarah had married Alderman William Cox when she was 15, very close to when Captain Kidd met her.

Kidd's courtship with Mrs. Oort was cut short in 1689 when war broke out between England and France and he took command of a privateering ship.

The laws of the time allowed the captain of a privateer vessel to capture those of the enemy and keep a substantial portion of the spoils of war. The share Kidd could obtain from privateering far exceeded what he might have hoped to earn by trading up and down the east coast of Newfoundland, Nova Scotia, and New England. He was undoubtedly enthusiastic over obtaining the commission.

Kidd was quite successful, capturing many ships in the West Indies. But in February 1690, while he was on shore in

Antigua to get water and supplies, his crew mutinied under the leadership of a renegade named Robert Culliford and set sail for New York, capturing and raiding other ships as they went.

Governor Codrington of Antigua felt compassion for Kidd's misfortune. He ruled that Kidd had given his crew no reason to mutiny and gave Kidd command of a recently captured French ship, renamed *Antigua*. Kidd chased his old ship, the *Blessed William,* all the way to New York, but just missed Culliford and his mutineers.

Probably because of his courtship with Sarah Oort, Kidd decided to remain in New York for a while and take a break from privateering.

Sarah's husband died on May 5, 1691, and Kidd wasted no time taking his place. Kidd and Sarah took out a marriage license just eleven days after Mr. Oort's demise.

Kidd substantially increased his wealth by the marriage. Sarah's real estate holdings were extensive and Kidd obtained what are now the most expensive properties in the world: 56 Wall Street, 86-90 and 119-21 Pearl Street, 52-56 Water Street, and 25, 27 and 29 Pine Street, all in downtown New York.

Still, Kidd continued his privateering career. In 1691 he captured a French ship for which he was awarded £150 by the governor and council of New York. But Kidd soon overstepped his privileges as a privateer. He sailed into a fleet of British and colonial ships and commandeered supplies, an act that was considered to border on piracy. Although Kidd maintained that he had the right under his privateer's commission to commandeer supplies, he lost his privateering license. This was probably the first of events to brand him a pirate.

Despite the loss of his commission, Kidd continued his life as a man of the sea. In 1695 he was given command of the brigantine *Arigo* and delivered a cargo to London. He gained the trust of several men of office, and soon the new governor of New York—Richard Coote, Earl of Bellomont—appointed him the leader of an antipiracy expedition backed by four of England's wealthiest and most prominent men. He was given a new ship of 287 tons and 34 guns. Christened the *Adventure Galley*, it set sail from Deptford on February 27, 1696.

Bad luck plagued Kidd from the beginning. He set out with seventy men, but twenty of them were quickly impressed into service on HMS *Duchess of Queensborough*. Kidd complained to Lord Admiral Russell at Sittingbourne and twenty men were sent, but they were not as valuable as the men he had lost; they lacked quality of seamanship and morals.

Enraged by the exchange of crew, Kidd set sail from Plymouth on April 23, 1696, for New York. Crossing the Atlantic, Kidd captured a French banker (a boat engaged in cod fishing on the Newfoundland banks) en route for Newfoundland and had it condemned in New York for £350.

Kidd recruited eighty-five more crew members, but these were of even more dubious character than his existing crew. They sailed down to the Indian Ocean, the raffish crewmembers increasingly hungry for plunder. Fearing that he might not be able to provide a return on the antipiracy expedition, and hoping to pacify his roguish crew, Kidd attacked a Moorish ship, *Mary*, off the West Indian coast. Its captain, an Englishman named Parker, was taken hostage to serve as a pilot due to his knowledge of the Malabar Coast.

With rumblings of mutiny increasing, Kidd apprehensively cruised up the Malabar Coast hoping desperately to encounter a pirate ship. It was during this excursion that Kidd committed an act that eventually led to his death: he scolded William Moore, the ship's gunner, for mumbling to himself about a failure to attack a passing Dutch ship. A quarrel ensued between the two and in the heat of the argument Kidd struck the gunner with a wooden bucket inflicting a mortal wound. The gunner died the following day.

Following William Moore's death, the *Adventure* continued up the coast. In November Kidd captured the Dutch ship *Rouparelle* and was delighted by the discovery that it was a French charter vessel, making the capture legal under his privateer's commission. But it wasn't much of a prize—its cargo consisted of baled cotton, some quilts, sugar, and two horses. Nevertheless, Kidd took his captured ship in tow and renamed it *November*.

Now Kidd's luck seemed to have finally turned, for on January 30, 1698, he captured the vessel *Quedah Merchant* carrying a rich cargo of silks, muslins, gold, jewels, sugar, iron, saltpeter, and guns. Its cargo has been estimated to have been worth between forty and seventy thousand pounds. Like his previous capture of the *Rouparelle,* the *Quedah* was also sailing under the authority of a French pass, making its capture legal. Kidd divided up the booty, set the *Quedah's* crew ashore, and headed for St. Mary's Island off the Madagascar Coast, with the *November* and *Quedah* now members of his fleet.

Kidd arrived at St. Mary's Island on April 1, 1698, and found the *Mocha*, a stolen East Indian frigate at anchor. To Kidd's surprise, it was commanded by his foe, Robert Culliford, who had led the mutiny aboard the *Blessed William.*

Kidd ordered an attack on the *Mocha* and a skirmish followed in which ninety-seven of his crew deserted to Culliford and then plundered the *November.* The *Mocha* then sailed away, leaving Kidd and his skeleton crew to complete his mission.

As the *Adventure* was leaking badly, Kidd stripped it of anything useful and burned the hull for its iron.

Kidd was now anxious to return home but the southwest monsoons blow in the Indian Ocean from April to October, so Kidd had no alternative but to sit and wait for the northwest trade winds of November.

While Kidd waited for the winds, the East Indian Company made complaints to the British Board of Trade regarding Indian Ocean piracies. In a sheath of reports laid before the board, Kidd's name was badly blackened. The British government decided to put an end to piracy by issuing an amnesty, and on December 8, 1698, a pardon was proclaimed to all pirates who would turn themselves in before April 30, 1699. The amnesty excluded Kidd and Captain John Avery (Long Ben), one of the most feared pirates of the day.

Kidd set sail for home on November 15, 1698, while—unbeknownst to him—colonial governors from Massachusetts to Jamaica were ordered to seize Kidd on sight.

When Kidd arrived in the Leeward Islands in April 1699, he learned that he had been denounced as a pirate and that orders for his arrest had been issued. If Kidd was to make it home without being captured he would have to ditch the *Quedah* in favour of a fast, anonymous ship.

At Mona Passage, Kidd purchased the sloop *Antonia* from a merchant by the name of Henry Bolton, transferred a portion of the *Quedah's* booty to the *Antonia*, moored the *Quedah* up a remote river in Hispaniola, and set sail for New York.

Kidd arrived in Long Island Sound in early June 1699 and waited offshore while his lawyer, James Emmott, tried to make arrangements with the governor of New York, Lord Bellomont, to have the warrant for arrest rescinded. Emmott gave the governor French passes from the *November* and *Quedah* to prove Kidd's innocence. The governor responded by writing a message to Kidd that a pardon could only be granted if he could provide satisfactory proof to refute the great variety of charges against him.

On receiving the letter, Kidd re-evaluated his position and decided to cache a portion of his booty as a bargaining tool. He buried a major load of gold and jewels in an orchard on Gardner's Island near the eastern end of Long Island Sound, with the permission of the island's owner, John Gardner. Gardner received some gifts and gave Kidd a receipt for the buried treasure.

Following his business on Gardner's Island, Kidd arrived in Boston to appear before Bellomont and the executive council, confident that the two French passes would gain him a pardon. But under Bellomont's orders, Kidd was arrested and thrown into Stone Prison on July 6, 1699.

The sponsors could only save themselves by making Kidd a scapegoat; the passes from the *Quedah* and the *Rouparelle* were conveniently disposed of. Now Kidd had no defence.

While Kidd was in prison, Bellomont had the loot on

Gardner's Island and the *Antonia* confiscated. The treasure was officially valued at fourteen thousand pounds.

After spending over a year in Stone Prison, Kidd was sent to England in February 1700 in the warship *Advice* to stand trial before the Admiralty Court. He was found guilty of piracy and the murder of his gunner, William Moore. The trial is said to have been "most irregular."

The trial was complicated by the fact that the four prominent and influential Englishmen who had backed Kidd and his antipiracy mission were politically embarrassed by his spiralling career. And, furthermore, Kidd had been enlisted by King William III under the Great Seal of England, and had become an embarrassment to the entire country.

On May 23, 1701, Captain William Kidd was hanged at Execution Dock, Wapping. He experienced a terrible death— the rope broke twice. The third time, however, it held. Kidd's body was dipped in tar and hung by chains beside the Thames River as a warning to all would-be pirates.

So after being a prominent citizen of New York City, Kidd became a criminal. But if he did indeed earn as much bounty as has been reported, and the treasure dug up at Gardner's Island was only worth fourteen thousand pounds, where did the *real* treasure end up? Most probably in Nova Scotia, many believe, and this belief has contributed immensely to his piratical fame, especially in this part of the world.

The 1759 founders of Chester, Nova Scotia, all heard stories of Kidd's exploits from their New England parents and grandparents who had lived in Kidd's day. They brought with them the legend of an old man in the New England Colonies of the 1600s, declaring on his deathbed that he had been a crew member of the notorious Captain William Kidd. He swore that many years earlier he, as a member of Kidd's crew, took part in the burying of a very large treasure on a secluded island somewhere off the coast, east of Boston. The founders of Chester were certain the treasure was in Nova Scotia.

Legends like this abound in the small coastal communities

of Nova Scotia. What follows is another favourite.

The settlers of a small Acadian village awoke one morning to find what they perceived to be a pirate ship anchored in their little harbour. Before them stood a band of grim-faced men who they took to be buccaneers from the evil in their eyes.

The ship had silently slipped into the harbour during the night. The crew had rowed quietly ashore, and now in the wee hours of the morning faced the frightened villagers.

But the visitors obviously had a problem. Their vessel was without masts.

The captain of the vessel turned out to be a charismatic individual who immediately won over the villagers with his charm. He described being caught in a violent storm and how all the masts and rigging had been torn off the ship. He said that neither he nor his crew had intentions of harming the people. Their only reason for being in the harbour was to repair their ship. He had chosen a fishing village because he suspected that some of the men there would be handy at boat building and repairs. He hoped that they would be able to make masts and help refit the vessel. He promised that no harm would come to the people while the work was being done as long as the men of the village cooperated. Furthermore, the work had to begin immediately and be carried out as quickly as possible. He stressed that although the men were not at liberty to refuse, he would pay generously for their labours.

The villagers worked long and hard, doing an excellent job of cutting and shaping new masts and making repairs. When the work was completed, the ship's skipper congenially called the villagers together and announced that he was none other than the infamous Captain William Kidd!

Kidd then offered payment for materials and labour but the superstitious villagers refused; the money was "tarnished with blood" and might bring them misfortune and tragedy.

Kidd didn't force payment on the villagers, knowing that they were god-fearing souls. But as he sailed away he tossed bars of silver and gold overboard, expecting the people to pick them up when he was gone. The villagers, however, would not touch the pirates' spoils, those ill-gotten gains.

Beyond legend, there was activity that lends substance to a widespread belief that Kidd spent a lot of—largely undocumented—time in Atlantic Canada. Kidd's crew of the *Blessed William,* who mutinied under Robert Culliford, sailed straight for Nova Scotia from Antigua, stopping only at New York for a refit and sale of cargo. Apparently they knew their way there, having visited before with Captain Kidd. These runaway sea marauders arrived at Port-Royal, Nova Scotia, on June 16, 1690, plundering and burning houses and destroying livestock belonging to the settlers. They hanged two of the residents and burned a woman and her children inside her cottage. Then they sailed across the Bay of Fundy, back around Cape Sable, through the Strait of Canso to New Brunswick, and over to Newfoundland, sacking and pillaging villages as they went. These were not the movements of a crew unfamiliar with the area. The course Culliford and his crew took indicates an in-depth knowledge of the coast of Nova Scotia and Atlantic Canada as a whole.

So the overwhelming likelihood is that Kidd extensively travelled the isolated inlets and coves of Nova Scotia and Newfoundland. And who are we to dispute hundreds of years of legends about silver, gold, and jewels, all buried beneath the soil of Atlantic Canadian shores?

𝔅𝔞𝔯𝔱𝔥𝔬𝔩𝔬𝔪𝔢𝔴 𝔅𝔬𝔟𝔢𝔯𝔱𝔰,
Newfoundland's Surprise

The tale of the cunning Black Bart.

Many Newfoundland residents say that there are only two seasons in the year—winter and summer—because spring comes so late it is hardly noticeable, and summer seems to last late into the fall. Winter is long and trying, and summer, with its long days, is a time most enjoyed by all. This in fact applies to most of Atlantic Canada, but especially to Newfoundland, where summer days are seldom uncomfortably warm and are usually cool and pleasant. For this reason many traders, privateers and buccaneers of bygone days left the southern summer heat and sailed north toward Newfoundland.

It may have been the nice weather that initiated something unexpected at Trepassey Bay, Newfoundland, one day in 1720. Trepassey Bay, situated on the southern coast of the Avalon Peninsula between Mistaken Point and Cape Pine, was a favourite port of call. In Trepassey Harbour, twenty-two merchant ships, with some twelve hundred crew members, lay at anchor. The sailors frequented the pubs, courted the girls, and spent their hard-earned wages. Out on the water, men visited between ships, telling jokes and sea stories and socializing with mugs of rum.

No one raised an eyebrow when a ship sailed directly into the harbour with trumpets blaring and drums beating. To the village residents and the sailors of the anchored fleet, it was just another high-spirited vessel and crew in for supplies, trade, fresh water and a little rest and relaxation. They would have been terrified had they known that the newcomer was a pirate ship with thirty-two cannons, twenty-seven swivel guns and a crew of sixty cutthroats eager for plunder, all commanded by the infamous Bartholomew Roberts, better known as Black Bart.

Black Bart and his crew were up from the eastern coast of South America, and perhaps they had indeed been lured by Newfoundland's pleasant summer—but they certainly had other motivation. After much success in the southern regions, they had had a run-in with a Captain Rogers of Barbados, who had been sent with a twenty gun ship to capture Bart. A vicious battle ensued in which the pirates fought a bloody, two-hour battle with their opponent. There were heavy losses for both parties, but Bart was not in the game to lose. He escaped his pursuer and decided to head north to safer—as well as cooler—waters.

Along the way, at the Bay of Los Todos Santos, on the east coast of South America, Bart sighted a huge fleet of heavily loaded Portuguese ships anchored off shore. He recklessly sailed directly in among the great ships and dropped anchor among them as if he were there by privilege or authority. No questions were asked, so audacious was the performance.

After having settled down for some supposed reason—perhaps to wait for another vessel—Bart singled out a nondescript-looking little vessel. As if he were a member of the fleet, Bart invited the captain of the little ship on board for a social hour. After a drink or two, Bart made his situation and intent known. He announced that he was a highwayman of the sea, and intended no harm to the Portuguese captain. All the captain need do was reveal the location of the richest vessel in the fleet, and he would then be immediately returned safely to his little vessel. If he refused to comply he would be immediately executed. The terrified captain pointed out a large forty-gun ship with a crew of 150 men. It was a rich treasure ship. Bart then reneged on his promise to return the captain immediately to his own ship; instead, he manoeuvred over to the rich ship. The detained captain, under duress, hailed the captain of the great treasure ship, made some friendly small talk, and invited him aboard Bart's ship for refreshments. The ruse worked to a point, but soon the treasure ship captain began to suspect that something was wrong, seeing a lot of running about from stem to stern on the big Portuguese ship. Bart, suspecting a problem, opened fire. Boats filled with pirates rowed over to and boarded the treasure ship, and the invasion was successfully completed in short order. It was a rich haul—Bart and his marauders obtained an enormous hoard of gold, as well as many desirable commodities such as sugar and tobacco.

Which brings us back to the anchored fleet in Trepassey Harbour. The men of the fleet there paid no attention to Bart as he manoeuvred among them with trumpets blasting and drums beating—it appeared to be just fanfare. Then, all at once, it seemed as if the whole world was exploding. With Bart blasting away at one ship and then another, nearly the entire fleet was ablaze. Taken completely by surprise, the sailors ineffectively tried to stave off the pirate attack. Panic spread throughout the fleet and when the guns stopped firing, all but one ship was sinking or burning.

As the day wore on, more trading vessels sailed into the harbour, and Bart took each of them as they entered. By the end of the day, he had seized and looted four more merchant ships, for a total of twenty-six vessels captured, looted, or destroyed.

With no further gain to be had in the bay, the pirates rowed ashore and robbed the village, leaving a path of terrorized residents and plundered houses in their wake.

The lone ship that had survived the early morning attack was a fine Bristol galley. It was captured by Bart, renamed the *Royal Fortune*, and later exchanged for another he captured.

Leaving Trepassey Bay, Bart rounded Mistaken Point, and sailed up the coast as far as Cape Spear, south of St. John's. On this jaunt, his scoundrels partied day and night with numerous puncheons of rum stolen at Trepassey and looted every vessel they met along the way.

After reaching Cape Spear, well replenished with munitions and with holds full of dried and salted cod and other food supplies, Bart headed down to Nova Scotia, where he had raided a fishing fleet off Canso on his way up to Trepassey Bay. Bart visited Cape Breton, where he captured and plundered six large French ships, one of which was even greater than his recent acquisition, *Royal Fortune*. He added that fine ship to his fleet. Following this raid, Bart headed back to southern waters.

Bartholomew Roberts was born in Wales and went to sea at an early age. An intelligent sailor, he worked his way up to the station of ship's master. In 1719 he sailed for the coast of Guinea as master of the *Princess* to pick up a group of black slaves at Anamaboe.

When the *Princess* reached its destination, it was attacked and captured by the infamous pirate Howel Davis, another Welshman. Bart was taken aboard Davis's ship and was given no choice but to join the crew. Bart had no desire to adopt the life of a buccaneer but became used to the depraved profession as time went by.

On stopping at the Island of Princes, off the African coast, Davis ran into trouble that cost him his life. He devised a plan to capture the Island of Princes: he would invite the governor aboard, imprison him, and then invade and take over the island. It might have worked but the night before the governor was to visit, a black captive swam ashore and alerted the residents.

The next day, Davis and a small group of his more respectable-looking pirates went ashore, where they were ambushed and killed by the governor's soldiers.

On observing the slaughter, the remaining pirate crew weighed anchor, raised the sails, and returned to the high seas.

Being a well-respected former ship's master, Bart was chosen by the pirate crew to be their captain and leader. Then a plan was devised to avenge the loss of Captain Davis. They returned to the Island of Princes and a landing party of thirty men stormed ashore under cover of brisk gun fire from the ship. The soldiers at the fort fled into the forest and Bart's pirates captured the fort and disposed of its cannons by hauling them into the ocean. Having completed their mission, the pirates again returned to the open sea.

Pirate Black Bart had a few fascinating and unique aspects to his personality. Whenever he launched an attack, he dressed in a crimson waistcoat and breeches, a hat with a scarlet plume, and a jewelled cross dangling from a gold necklace.

Unlike most pirates, Bart never touched a drop of liquor— the strongest drink he would take was tea. He made his men retire every night at nine o'clock. He forbade any form of gambling on board his ships, including card-playing or dice-rolling. Women were not allowed on board his vessels. He forbade his men to take liberties with women, and if a sailor brought a woman on board and seduced her, Bart had him put to death.

Bart was also observant of religious matters. He didn't force any particular religious persuasion on his men, but his musicians were always given a period of rest on Sundays.

It was normal for pirate captains to press captured crew members into service, but Bart never forced a man to join the piratical fraternity against his will.

Following the episode at the Island of Princes, Bart carried out a campaign of pillage unmatched by any other pirate in the history of buccaneering. In less than three years, he captured more than four hundred ships.

Captain Bart's last encounter with another ship took place on February 10, 1722. Bart had entered a bay of a West Indian island to careen his ships when a British warship, the *Swallow*, unexpectedly arrived. Its captain had Bart on his list of culprits to be apprehended. When Bart and his crew noticed the man-of-war slowly creeping into the bay, they knew that trouble was in store. There was no way to escape, so Bart pulled anchor and struck out to engage the *Swallow*.

A vicious battle took place in which neither side gained an advantage. Bart stood on deck wearing his most valuable garments of colourful fabric, and flaunted several handsomely carved pistols. And while he directed operations, dressed in his finest garb, a burst of grapeshot hit the pirate vessel and Bart was shot through the throat. Grasping his neck, which was bubbling blood, he dropped dead on the deck.

Without Bart to lead them, the pirates ceased fire, threw down their weapons and surrendered.

It was Bart's command to his crew that, should he ever be killed in battle, he be tossed overboard to the sharks. On that day in 1722, he received his wish.

Captain Bartholomew is unique in the annals of buccaneering—why did a man who made his living by stealing have such a strict moral code for himself and his crew? And how did an unwillingly impressed crew member become a highly skilled pirate captain so quickly?

Certainly the people of Trepassey Bay, Newfoundland, never forgot the display of his skill on a cool summer's day in their harbour.

Samuel Hall, the Annapolis Valley Terror

Hall's Harbour is named after this ruthless pirate.

One day in the spring of 1779, a serious meeting was held by an angry group of Annapolis Valley, Nova Scotia, residents. Those in attendance were settlers with farms near the southern foot of North Mountain. The gathering consisted largely of young and middle-aged men and a few of their wives. Some were bitterly angry, others frustrated and frightened, and most were all three. And for good reason. News had reached them that the pirate, Captain Samuel Hall, was back in the Bay of Fundy. His presence could mean another raid on their farms.

Captain Hall wrought terror in the hearts of these valley settlers. With a pirate crew from the New England colonies, he would sneak from the bay across the mountain in the evening, and swoop down on the unsuspecting valley residents in the wee hours of the morning, pillaging farm after farm.

The villagers in the valley were a hard-working and thrifty lot. Their splendid barns and chicken coops teamed with livestock and their root cellars were always well-stocked with vegetables for the long, cold, winter months. And they were generous, for they often shared the products of their labour with the Mi'kmaq when hunting was hampered by deep snow.

Captain Hall also pretended to be generous. He handed out much-desired gifts to the Mi'kmaq such as iron pots, hatchets, iron arrow points, blankets, and an array of cheap, glittering jewellery. But his handouts came with a price. As the Mi'kmaq were accustomed to visiting the villagers and begging for food during the cold winter months, Captain Hall persuaded them to take note of where supplies were stored, and to share this information with him.

The villagers who met that day in 1779 suspected that the Mi'kmaq were working for Captain Hall, but what could be done? Threatening the Mi'kmaq with violence would be ineffective; they would not take the villagers seriously. Threatening to cut off all support during the winter would appear miserly and mean. What they had to do was clear: they would simply offer the Mi'kmaq more than Captain Hall could.

There was a Mi'kmaw encampment between the village and the Bay of Fundy. A couple of the men who spoke the aboriginals' language left immediately and sealed a new verbal agreement. The better bribe required that the Mi'kmaq immediately notify the villagers when Captain Hall's ship, the *Mary Jane*, arrived in their region of the bay, and that they help with an attack on Captain Hall and his crew. In return, the villagers promised a whole winter's food supply—far more than anything handed out by Captain Hall.

One of Captain Hall's favourite anchorages in the Bay of Fundy was a small harbour near the mouth of a brook that spills out of North Mountain. (The brook and the harbour now both bear the Captain's last name.) It was from this anchorage that Captain Samuel Hall and his band of cutthroats crossed over the mountain and pillaged the poor, hardworking settlers in the valley below.

Although not exceptionally well sheltered, the harbour offered Captain Hall and his marauders privacy, as there were no settlers there. It provided an alternative to sailing into the populated Minas Basin, where the ship's presence would have been spotted by residents and reported to the authorities in Halifax. It was a safe anchorage for the *Mary Jane*: frequent fogs in the snug little harbour hid the vessel from warships whose masters would have liked nothing more than to capture Captain Hall and his pirate gang. Also, the nearest village lay in the valley on the opposite side of the mountain, far enough away that there was little fear of the *Mary Jane* being noticed by a villager. And the Mi'kmaw encampment situated between the harbour and the village provided further security.

On board the *Mary Jane*, however, lurked a threat to that security. It was a situation that would erupt into near catastrophe for Captain Hall and his sea brigands. The cabin boy had fallen in love with the daughter of the chief that Captain Hall made his deals with. The two lovers had met on one of Captain Hall's frequent visits, and they saw each other whenever the *Mary Jane* dropped anchor in the little harbour.

Captain Hall was aware of the cabin boy's romance with the chief's daughter. He knew that the boy would be eager to visit the Mi'kmaw encampment as soon as possible each time the *Mary Jane* visited the bay, and so he seized the opportunity to use the boy as his messenger. The cabin boy's visits to the encampment announced the ship's arrival, and he would be asked if supplies on the ship were low, if Captain Hall had gifts to distribute, or if the captain had instructions for the chief, and so on.

As well as being in love with the Mi'kmaw girl, the cabin boy had become close friends with her younger brother. The two boys played games and exchanged knowledge—what one boy knew well was often a mystery to the other. Indeed, it was a happy time for all three youth whenever the *Mary Jane* sailed into the harbour. But those happy days were not to last.

Not long after the villagers negotiated the deal with the Mi'kmaq, Captain Samuel Hall and his cutthroat crew slid into the harbour for a few days of rest from plunder on the high seas. A lookout reported the arrival of the *Mary Jane* to the Mi'kmaw chief, who immediately sent his daughter to notify the villagers. In view of the relationship of the chief's daughter and son with the cabin boy, no-one told them of the change in dealings with Captain Hall. As the girl hurried towards the village, she wondered why her father had dispatched her to tell the villagers of the return of the ship that her lover had just arrived on. But it was not her place to ask questions, so she ran her errand knowing that the cabin boy from the *Mary Jane* would arrive at the encampment while she was gone, and hoping that he would still be there when she returned.

The cabin boy did indeed arrive, looking for his sweetheart. He told the chief that the *Mary Jane* was short on food supplies and that an attack on the village was to be undertaken that evening; he then received information on the best-stocked barns. Then he waited for the girl. Several hours elapsed but his love did not return. Finally, when he could wait no longer, he asked the girl's brother to pass on a message to her: he would be alone on the *Mary Jane* that evening during the attack, waiting for her to come to him.

At dusk the girl returned, hoping that her lover would still be waiting. When she found that he had left, she cried bitter tears, until her brother told her that she was to go to the harbour and meet the cabin boy on the shore, where she would be ferried over to the ship. She hurried down the mountainside to meet her lover who, as promised, was waiting for her on the beach near the *Mary Jane*.

Meanwhile, the girl's brother happened to overhear the men

of the tribe discussing the settlers' plan to raid Captain Hall and his crew—it was to take place that very evening! Captain Hall and his men were to be ambushed on their way over the hills from the village. This was shocking news to the boy, and he became concerned for the safety of his sister and his friend. He had to find a way of slipping out of the camp unnoticed and getting down to the ship.

The boy waited for his chance while the men became engrossed in storytelling around the campfire; during a moment of great hilarity, the boy slipped away and raced over the hills towards the harbour.

As he approached the shore, he heard the pirates from the *Mary Jane* noisily making their way up the hillside from the beach: there was no need for silence until they passed the Mi'kmaw encampment and were approaching the village. He rushed into their midst, grabbed Captain Hall by the arm and rapidly told him of the trap that had been set to capture and kill him and his men. But the boy was too late.

Assisted by a couple of Mi'kmaw guides, the settlers had manoeuvred themselves behind the advancing pirates. Concealed by the pirate gang's noisy trekking through the brush, they had silently crept between them and the ship. Shots rang out, piercing the tranquillity of the night. Realizing that they were outmanoeuvred and perhaps far outnumbered by the villagers, Hall and his ratty followers broke rank and ran for cover into the surrounding woods.

The settlers followed them into the forest, but as they searched the thickets, the Mi'kmaw boy intervened. He skilfully rounded up the pirates and led them to the rear of their pursuers. Even as he helped the pirates, however, another party of settlers from the village was making its way down the hillside towards the *Mary Jane*. They were determined to catch and kill Captain Hall and his band of cutthroats.

Back on the *Mary Jane*, the cabin boy and his sweetheart heard the noise of gunfire ringing out from the woods. They knew that something had gone dreadfully wrong.

Captain Hall and his men were obviously under attack.

As he had done on previous raids, Captain Hall had left his cabin boy in charge of the ship's treasure chest—a small, iron-bound box said to be filled with gold and precious jewels. Captain Hall's instructions were that if he and his men didn't return by a certain time, the cabin boy was to bury the chest in the sands close to the edge of the woods. If the captain and crew should fail to return, the treasure would be the boy's, as no one else would know of its existence. That would be the cabin boy's reward for faithful and trustworthy service.

Obeying Captain Hall's instructions, the cabin boy and his sweetheart lowered the treasure chest down into a rowboat and rowed it to shore. As they dragged the heavy chest along the beach, some of the ambushing settlers heard the footsteps on the beach stones and opened fire. The cabin boy dropped dead with the first volley, his blood splattering over the treasure chest as he fell face down on the beach. Another burst of fire claimed the life of the girl. She lay face up by the cabin boy's side, her lifeless eyes staring at a star-studded sky.

The settlers rushed up to examine their kill. They were stunned when they saw the blood-soaked corpses of a male youth and a young girl. Although greed eclipsed the tragedy for a moment, and a couple of the settlers seized the treasure chest and began dragging it back towards the woods that bordered the beach, they soon discovered that the chest was sticky with blood. The superstitious among them feared the blood-covered chest of pirate treasure and wasted no time in ridding themselves of their evil acquisition. They hastily dug a hole in the sand and buried the chest of gold and jewels.

Glad to have disposed of the blood-covered chest, they went back into the woods to join the others but couldn't find them. The chief's son had cleverly guided the pirates away from the searching settlers to the anchored *Mary Jane*.

Giving little thought to the whereabouts of his cabin boy or the treasure chest, Captain Hall hastily pulled anchor and sailed out of the harbour.

The following day, the chief's son found the dead bodies

of his sister and the cabin boy. He buried the cabin boy near a large rock on the shore, not far from the edge of the forest. Then he carried the dead body of his sister back to the encampment.

The boy, his family, and all residents of the camp were deeply saddened by the tragedy. The villagers were satisfied with the results of their undertaking but deeply disturbed by the unintentional shooting of the chief's daughter. It was a high price to pay for driving off the pilfering Samuel Hall.

For his part, Captain Hall did not return to the village that year, nor the next, nor the next….Captain Samuel Hall never once returned to the harbour that now bears his name.

The settlers did not forget the buried treasure chest, but were initially too superstitious to cross back over the mountain and dig it up. Years later, some of the settlers lost a little of their fear and went to the harbour to recover the treasure, but no one could remember *exactly* where it had been buried. They searched and searched but the treasure was never found.

And the treasure was forever lost, but not so the horrid memory of the infamous Captain Samuel Hall.

𝕿𝖍𝖔𝖒𝖆𝖘 𝕻𝖔𝖚𝖓𝖉,
Pirate for a Noble Cause

Not all pirates were motivated by greed alone.

Sir Edmund Andros, governor of the Dominion of New England, sat on the edge of his hard bed in the confinement quarters of Boston Castle Island and wiped away the sweat that was blinding him as he tried to read in the intense August heat. Salt from the sweat stung his eyes. The only relief from the discomfort was to lay his book aside and close his eyes. As he sat with eyes closed, sweat flowing from his brow, Andros pondered his unfortunate situation.

It was August 2, 1689. He had been held prisoner for about three and a half months, having been placed under arrest and taken to the island on April 18.

Night and day, Andros had gone over the events leading up to his imprisonment. They were complicated. The colonial government had lost control over the people of Massachusetts and there was much unrest. A group of rebel New England citizens had captured and imprisoned Andros after receiving news that King James II had been removed from the throne and William of Orange had entered England as the new king. Now, the governor placed all his hope for freedom on the anticipated efforts of a Boston Harbour cartographer, Thomas Pound.

Andros had arrived from England in December 1686 as the new Governor. In May of the following year, he had sent the frigate *Rose*, commanded by Captain John George, up the east coast as far as Pemaquid (about forty miles northeast of Portland, Maine) to check on the safety of commercial shipping; piracy was a major concern. The pilot of the expedition was Thomas Pound, an expert cartographer and mariner.

Sir Edmund Andros had been at Pemaquid with an army of a thousand soldiers when news of the royal proclamation of William of Orange hit town. He returned to Boston, a rebellion against him began, and he and Captain George were made prisoners.

Thomas Pound and his colleagues had worked out an escape plan for him. Some of the guards were Andros sympathizers, and were to set him free to slip away to Rhode Island. In the meantime, Pound and crew would sail out of Boston Harbour and perform acts of piracy, capturing and plundering ships off the coast, causing the government frigate *Rose* to sail out and pursue them. And here was a twist to the plan: the crew of the *Rose* were also Andros sympathizers and would team up with Pound and sail to Rhode Island, where Andros would be waiting. Once aboard, the two vessels would sail to France and Andros would try to assist his deposed monarch.

Unfortunately, the beautifully planned escape did not work out. The governor did make his initial escape from Castle Island on August 3, 1689, but he was captured a few days later and returned to the island. Early in the morning on August 8,

Thomas Pound and a small crew, unaware that the governor had been captured and returned to Castle Island, set sail in a Bermuda-type vessel owned by a Thomas Hawkins, who held the position of sailing master, and commanded by Pound.

Far out in the bay, they dropped their sails and floated silently off the shores of an island and waited. They heard the sound of a boat being hauled off the shore and into the water, and soon a row boat came upon the scene. It was manned by five heavily armed men. They rowed up to the side of the Bermuda craft, and Pound threw them a line. Tying up to the side of the vessel, they climbed aboard. Pound had now added five able fighting men complete with guns and ammunition to his crew. With his extra crewmen assigned to their individual tasks, Pound struck out on an easterly course.

The first vessel Pound encountered was a small fishing sloop, but he didn't capture and plunder the vessel. All he did was purchase some fish and borrow a few extra gallons of fresh water—certainly not an act of piracy.

Continuing onward, Pound fell in with the ketch *Mary*, commanded by a Captain Chard and with a crew of four. He was heading home with a cargo of fish. Pound took over the ketch, and a few days later moved Hawkins and the entire pirate crew over to the *Mary* and let Captain Chard and two of his crew go free. One of the remaining men, John Darby, volunteered to join Pound; the other was impressed.

As soon as Captain Chard returned home he reported the piratical episode and a vessel was sent out to capture Pound—but it was to no avail. By the time the marines put out to sea, the *Mary* was well on its way up the coast. The marines returned home empty-handed.

Pound's plan was to obtain more men for his crew, preferably soldiers or marines: fighting men, with arms and ammunition. To this end, he dropped anchor in Casco Bay a few miles off from the bay's fortress, with the hope of finding military men at the fort who were not in favour of the rebellion against Governor Andros and would join Pound's crew. Three of his men were sent by longboat to the fort on the pretence of acquiring fresh water. After filling their casks they struck up a conversation with a couple of soldiers and learned that the fort's physician was not in favour of the rebellion. With that good news, they told the fort's commanding officer that they had been attacked by pirates and that their captain had been badly injured and needed a doctor. The commander could see the vessel anchored off in the distance and agreed.

When the physician went aboard the *Mary*, he didn't find a wounded captain and asked what was the meaning of his visit. Pound gave the doctor a full run-down on the scheme to help Governor Andros escape to France and asked him to round up some men from the fort to join the crew of the *Mary*. He also asked the physician to join the pirate crew as "ship's doctor." The physician was tempted by the latter request, thought the invitation over, and declined. However, he was an Andros sympathizer and agreed to try and recruit soldiers at the fort.

Returning to the fort, the physician talked with men he could trust not to tattle to the commander. Many were afraid to desert their posts, but he was successful in finding seven soldiers prepared to join the crew of the *Mary*.

The commander noticed the doctor chatting with various soldiers, and became suspicious—the medical man appeared to have something up his sleeve. It made the commander nervous and that evening he placed a greater number of men than usual in the guard around the fort.

The seven soldiers were among the men on guard duty. Late that night, when all was quiet and most were asleep, the seven soldiers helped themselves to guns and ammunition, stole a small boat, and rowed out to the *Mary*, where they were welcomed aboard and joined the pirate crew.

With his additional armed crew, Pound hauled anchor and headed down the coast. Off of Cape Cod, he fell in with and captured a sloop named *Goodspeed*, commanded by a Captain John Smart and bound for Nantucket Island, east of Martha's Vineyard, Massachusetts. Pound transferred over to the *Goodspeed* and gave the *Mary* to Captain Smart, urging him to go directly to Boston and report the piratical caper.

He hoped to raise the wrath of the government to the point where they would send out the *Rose* and the original plan of uniting with the government frigate could be completed.

On reaching Boston, Captain Smart had plenty to tell and he passed on a message from Pound that challenged the government to pursue him, egging on the authorities with a threat that they would be met with inordinately fierce resistance because Pound and every man in the crew would fight until death rather than be taken alive. In effect, he dared the government to pursue him.

Infuriated, the government went out in pursuit. Pound waited for the *Rose* with baited breath. Teaming up with the *Rose* and its crew of Andros sympathizers was vital to the plan. A sail appeared in the distance and Pound fully expected to greet the government frigate, but, to his dismay, the sloop *Resolution* appeared in his spy glass. Fortunately, the wind was in Pound's favour. Hoisting every square inch of canvas, Pound and his men left the *Resolution* far behind and made good their escape.

After picking up some fresh meat at Cape Cod, Pound headed down the coast towards Martha's Vineyard. On the way, he spotted a sail on the horizon and took off after the vessel. It was the brigantine *Merrimack* out of Newbury, Massachusetts. The brigantine's captain, John Kent, put up little resistance when he saw the pirate emblem flying from the *Mary*. Pound was short on stores and only robbed the vessel of food and supplies. Then he let Captain Kent and his brigantine go free.

Now, Pound ran into bad luck with the weather. A strong wind out of the northeast pounded the *Mary* day after day, driving her more than four hundred miles off course, down to Chesapeake Bay, Virginia. While in the bay, Pound sailed up the York River and recruited a few more men. After that, he headed back for the coast of Massachusetts.

Arriving at Naushon Island, in Vineyard Sound, the largest of the Elizabeth Islands of Buzzard Bay, Pound entered Tarpaulin Cove, a favoured sheltered harbour, and took on fresh water. A few days later he chased a small vessel into Martha's Vineyard

Harbour, where it was defended by the residents. A fight between the pirates and inhabitants of the harbour took place, at which point Pound gave up and headed back out to sea. But while the fight was raging, several Bostonians who were in the harbour village at the time recognized Thomas Hawkins, sailing master and owner of the ship Pound commanded. They warned him never to return to Boston, for if he did, he would surely be hanged for piracy. This worried Hawkins, and a few days later, on reaching Race Point, near Cape Cod, he jumped ship, hoping that if he hid out for a while, the Bostonians would forget that they saw him with the pirates.

After attacking a couple of vessels and robbing them of salt pork, cheese, beef, butter, peas, and corn, Pound returned to Tarpaulin Cove. Meanwhile, the governor in Boston received news of Pound's fight with the inhabitants of Martha's Vineyard Harbour and sent out Captain Samuel Pease with Lieutenant Benjamin Gallop and twenty marines to apprehend the pirates. The avengers sailed to Cape Cod in the first week of October and then went on down to Woods Hole, where they were told that Pound was anchored in Tarpaulin Cove. Woods Hole is not far from Tarpaulin, and Captain Pease set out at once in high spirits. Excitement among the marines ran high as they anticipated catching and bringing home the sea marauders. They cleaned and lubricated their musket gun barrels, checked their individual supplies of ammunition, and sharpened their cutlasses. They were eager and ready to take on and capture the hateful culprits of the deep.

Pound had just pulled anchor and was heading out of Tarpaulin Cove when Captain Pease and Lieutenant Gallop sailed in with the marines. Pound and his crew were completely taken by surprise and there was no escape route. They had no alternative but to stand up to their assailants.

The marines struck with an unprecedented ferocity and Pound and his ruffians, although unprepared for a fierce battle, fought back with unparalleled tenacity. The roar of gunfire was horrific, and neither side gained an advantage. The two vessels drew closer and blood spouted from gunshot wounds as the marines and pirates exchanged musket fire. Shrill cries of pain mingled with the roar of the gun fire. Smoke and gun powder swirled over the vessels. It was a desperate and bloody fight, and it grew considerably worse. As the battle progressed, the marines threw their grapnels onto the pirate sloop and clambered aboard.

The pirates fought until either dead or too injured to swing a cutlass or pull a trigger. They fought ferociously, without consideration for their lives, because capture would only result in a trip to the gallows. They thought it better to die out there on the water than spend months in a hell-hole prison cell, followed by the hangman's noose.

The battle ended when every pirate was either dead or severely wounded. Thomas Pound was seriously injured; one pirate received no less than seven wounds in his arms; another was shot in both legs, another was shot in the jaw; a bullet entered the ear and punched out the eye of yet another. The tally: fourteen wounded and six killed. All but two of the wounded were in serious condition.

The attack force also suffered serious losses. Captain Pease was severely wounded and died a short time later. Although the two sides were more or less evenly matched in numbers, the marines fared better and a sufficient number were still standing when the battle ended to put the injured pirates in irons.

Pound and his wounded men were taken to Boston and thrown into prison. The doctor who attended to the pirates' wounds apparently put in many long hours: his bill came to more than twenty-one pounds at a time when one pound a month was a substantial income for a tradesman. The amount of his bill, presuming that it was not inflated, indicates the seriousness of the injuries and the time required by the doctor to mend the wounds.

Thomas Hawkins drew up enough courage to return to Boston and was the first to arrive. He was arrested, thrown into prison, and tried on January 9, 1690 for piracy and found guilty. Next came Pound and the remaining pirates. On

January 17, 1690, Thomas Pound and three other pirates were pronounced guilty of piracy and murder, and sentenced to be hanged. But not all the sentences were carried out. One of the magistrates that tried the pirates, Waitstill Winthrop, had a brother who was married to a sister of Thomas Hawkins. Magistrate Winthrop pronounced that the verdict was unfair and obtained signatures from numerous influential Bostonians on a petition to pardon Pound, Hawkins, and another convicted man, Eleazer Buck. All three received a respite and, several weeks later, Pound was reprieved at the request of several prominent Boston women. Eventually, all but one of Thomas Pound's surviving crew escaped the gallows. The hanged man was Thomas Johnson, a waterfront undesirable known as the "limping privateer." Some contemporaries believed he was only killed to satisfy the large crowd that had gathered at the gallows on the day of the scheduled hanging of Pound and his ruffians.

In the spring of 1690, Thomas Pound and Thomas Hawkins signed on the government frigate *Rose* as crew on a voyage to England. En route the *Rose* was attacked by a French vessel, and might have been captured and plundered except for the intervention of another English ship. It joined the battle and helped defeat the French attacker. All three crews suffered heavy losses. Over a hundred of the Frenchmen were killed and numerous others wounded but despite this disastrous loss, the French captain managed to sail his ship away without being taken. Both Thomas Hawkins and Captain John George lost their lives in the battle.

Thomas Pound survived and reached England unscathed. By then Sir Edmund Andros was also in England, having been released from captivity on Boston's Castle Island. Pound communicated with him and, probably through Andros' recommendation, was made commander of the frigate *Sally Rose* in early August of 1690.

Following his return to England Sir Edmund Andros was appointed Governor of Virginia, and his loyal friend and patriot,

Thomas Pound, was well rewarded. After being stationed off the Virginia Coast, he retired as a gentleman in a community near London, England.

Thomas Pound died in 1703, fourteen years after he set out to aid the Governor of New England in his attempt to escape from captivity on Boston's Castle Island.

The Piratical Mystery of
Isle Haute

Is there

still treasure

buried

on the Bay

of Fundy

island?

The lighthouse keeper of Isle Haute, John Fullerton, stood alone on the ocean pier, watching the tiny speck in the distance grow larger. Unlike most days on the Bay of Fundy, there was hardly any swell. The object of his watchful eye, Captain Dewis's small fishing boat, was making good time as it crossed the sometimes treacherously rough thirteen-mile stretch of water separating Isle Haute from Advocate Harbour on the Nova Scotia mainland.

Captain Dewis killed the engine as he brought his small fishing boat within an arm's reach of a tall ladder on the side of the high pier. Fullerton skillfully caught the bow-line and secured it to a cleat. The captain waited onboard while three passengers—Fullerton's wife, Margaret, his fifteen-year-old son, Donald, and a new visitor to the island, a heavyset man with thick wavy hair—nimbly climbed the ladder and stepped aboard the pier deck.

After unloading luggage and equipment, Captain Davis returned to the mainland and Mrs. Fullerton introduced the visitor to her husband. The newcomer was Edward Rowe Snow, an American resident of Marshfield, Massachusetts, and famous author of books on pirate tales and treasure lore. Fullerton's wife and son had met Snow at his hotel in Advocate Harbour and helped arrange transportation to the Island with Captain Davis.

Although Snow and Fullerton had just met, they weren't really strangers. They had corresponded by mail. The year was 1952 and Snow had decided he wanted to visit the island early that summer, but had encountered barriers when planning his trip. He learned that there was no public transportation system linking the island with the mainland; nor was there a hotel or guest home on the island. However, there was a lighthouse where he might be able to stay, and fishermen who would take him over to the island. Snow made arrangements and Fullerton wrote that he and his wife would be most happy to provide food and lodging at the lighthouse during his visit.

Snow had made the reason for his visit clear: He wasn't particularly interested in the fauna, the geology, or the ecology of the island. He was visiting in search of pirate treasure!

Isle Haute would in fact be an ideal place for a pirate to hide booty: the forty- to fifty-foot tides hinder access to the island, and the three hundred-foot-high rocky cliffs challenge the visitor to reach the top. The French explorer Samuel de Champlain discovered Isle Haute during his voyage of 1604 and named it for its height—*haute* being French for "high."

In an account written by Snow after his visit to Isle Haute, he tells of first hearing about the Island in 1945 from Leland C. Bickford of the Yankee Network News Service. Bickford told of an amazing "cliff-island" in the Bay of Fundy off the coast of Nova Scotia where the "cliffs rose sheer out of the sea."

Bickford went on to tell of a treasure purportedly buried near a large rock on the Island.

Snow further reports that he received a letter in 1949 from "an enthusiastic Canadian" who was convinced that there was a substantial pirate treasure "within thirty miles of Advocate Harbour, Nova Scotia." Snow agreed that if he found treasure in that vicinity he would share a portion with the gentleman who gave him the information. But it was not until 1952 that he identified an old map he had purchased in 1947 as a pirate treasure chart of Isle Haute and decided to go to the island and search for treasure.

The map that Snow purchased has an outline almost identical to Isle Haute and bears the island's name. It shows a lake at the east end of the island, and an arrow with the words "The Place" points to a spot a short distance east of the lake. At the bottom of the map there is the notation "Victoria, 23758 P/8, 1355 G, E. Low." Snow writes that the map was reproduced from one prepared by or for the notorious pirate Edward Low. He presumed that "Victoria" refers to a ship that Low had captured called *the Nostra Signiora de Victoria* of Portugal. Snow notes that the original map was examined by experts who found that it was drawn on seventeenth-century paper.

Early in the morning of June 23, 1952, Snow packed his gear, which included a metal detector along with picks and shovels, and struck out for Advocate, Nova Scotia, and Isle Haute, accompanied by his wife Anna-Myrle and their daughter Dorothy. He had expected to take his wife and daughter with him over to the island but was advised on his arrival that he should leave them behind because of the unpredictable weather conditions in the region. He was told that they could be stranded on the island for an indefinite length of time should bad weather set in. Both his wife and daughter were disappointed, but respected the advice of the fishermen of Advocate. Arrangements were made for them to stay ashore as guests of the family of the former Isle Haute lighthouse keeper, Don Morris, while Snow was on the Island.

On the trip over to the island, Snow discovered that he was

not the first man to come to Isle Haute in search of treasure. Dougald Carmichael of Vancouver, British Columbia, had visited the island at least twice, once in 1925 and again in 1929.

Snow also learned of an uncommissioned lighthouse helper, Dave Spicer, who still came and left the island at his own whim. Spicer was an unusual character, as Snow learned from the lighthouse keeper. That evening Fullerton told Snow that on several occasions a headless ghost appeared before Dave Spicer. Although visitors had occasionally explored the island, and the Fullertons were always very active on and around its shores, only Dave had ever seen the spirit.

According to Snow, there is a legend that Edward Low beheaded an unruly buccaneer when the pirate crew went ashore, which would explain the ghost's residency on the island.

After breakfast on the day following his arrival, Edward Snow began his treasure hunt at the eastern end of the lake, where his map's arrow pointed to "The Place." At first he only found pieces of a chain and rusted iron with his metal detector. Then he came upon a pit that he assumed had been dug years before by another treasure hunter. It was about eight feet long by three feet wide, and about two and a half feet deep. After probing the pit with his metal detector, Snow picked up a strong reaction on the southwest corner wall. He dug a little beyond the southwest corner of the pit and found an iron spike. Tossing the spike aside, he continued to dig and was soon rewarded. First he uncovered the ribs of a human skeleton and then a human skull. By now night had set in, so he postponed further digging until the morning and returned to the lighthouse where he fascinated the Fullertons with his story.

Around eight o'clock the next morning Snow headed back down towards the lake, accompanied by Fullerton and his son, Donald, with Mrs. Fullerton some distance in the lead. Snow writes, "We started down over the cliff and reached a point where we could look half a mile away and see where we had been digging. John Fullerton was the first to notice what apparently was a man standing half in and half out of the pit. Donald and I also saw the figure, and the three of us were baffled by it, as we were sure that there was no one else on the island at the time. Nor had any fishing boat come to the Island to let anyone ashore. A moment later the figure appeared to stand away from the pit, holding something high in his left hand." They hurried down to the pit but there was nobody in sight when they arrived. They searched around the Island and up and down the shores but found no one. The Fullertons thought that it might be Dave but when questioned he swore that he had not been near the pit by the lake on that day. Had the family finally seen the ghost Dave Spicer knew well?

On returning to the pit, Snow uncovered more skeletal remains. Removing the soil from an arm, wrist and fingers, he began picking coins from the soil. In his account of the discovery, Snow writes: "Again and again my fingers sifted through the dirt seeking and finding the hard metal objects until I had quite a collection in my possession. After digging down a full eighteen inches, I tried to get a reaction with the metal detector, but there was no further response." Satisfied with his find, Snow packed up his gear and returned to the mainland. His find consisted of valuable gold and silver coins of rare Spanish and Portuguese mintage, and at least one was dated 1710.

Fullerton told Snow that Dougald Carmichael, the treasure hunter who visited the island in the 1920s, had sold stocks in his venture. In 1929, he arrived at the lighthouse excitedly announcing that he had hit pay dirt. He claimed to have uncovered both gold and jewels. Then, shortly after announcing his discovery, Carmichael left the island and never returned.

Fullerton told Snow that many people had searched for pirate treasure on the island, and that the favourite locations for searching were near the eastern end of the lake and in the vicinity of a large rock beside the road leading up the hill to the lighthouse. Carmichael first dug in the former location, and claimed to find treasure in the latter.

Fullerton also told Snow that an ancient axe had recently been found near a small swampy pond on a high part of the Island. It was supposedly left there by a visitor of long ago. Snow wondered if perhaps the axe had belonged to pirate Edward Low.

Carmichael had either lied about finding treasure or was greedy for more. A news article in the September 9, 1931 edition of the *Berwick Register* titled: "Will Search for Captain Kidd's Treasure on Isle Haute: Much Sought Treasure Trove Believed Buried in Lake on Island in Bay of Fundy," stated that Dougald Carmichael was once again seeking Captain Kidd's treasure on Isle Haute. His address was given as Advocate, Cumberland County, but one would assume that this was the same Dougald Carmichael said to have been a resident of Vancouver. The article told of a plan to drain a small lake on the island so that the treasure, consisting of gold and jewels, could be recovered. It told the following story:

The Advocate man is 82 years of age and at one time was station master of Hamilton, N. B. He was in the Northwest rebellion and was wounded, and was a visitor to Vancouver when that city was nothing but a camping site. Mr. Carmichael first learned of the alleged Kidd treasure being on Isle Haute from ancestors who are said to have secured first hand information from a member of Kidd's crew. The sailor is said to have declared that he saw the gold and jewels landed and placed in the lake, which was then scheduled two fathoms deep. With a man named McCready, Mr. Carmichael started for Isle Haute to reclaim the treasure. Their efforts failed because of the water and sand that drifted into the lake and buried the chest of gold and jewels, it is believed. Some of these jewels came from South America, he declares and he refuses to allow a steam shovel to be used to dredge the lake in fear that some of these valuable jewels might be damaged.

The article went on to describe a strange marble slab found

on the beach of Isle Haute when the lighthouse was under construction. It was cut into a "three-corned shape" and inscribed with the words "R. Kidd 5 fathoms east and two fathoms deep." The slab was cut in the exact shape of the lake at the east end of the island. The slab's inscription was exactly in accordance with the "location said to have been told by the member of Kidd's crew to Mr. Carmichael's ancestor."

Many questions remain after the searches conducted by Dougald Carmichael and the treasure uncovered by Edward Snow. Did Captain Kidd and Edward Low both bury treasure on Isle Haute? If so, did Carmichael find it? There were those who declared that Carmichael had indeed found Kidd's loot, and those who had been present throughout the digging and swore that nothing had been found. Carmichael never reported finding a penny to the Government, which may explain the denials—a treasure trove law required a kickback of ten percent to the Crown.

Why didn't Snow return to Isle Haute and continue his search? According to his treasure map, there was a vast fortune remaining to be uncovered. Perhaps Snow believed that the treasure he found was a leftover portion, and that Carmichael had already found the bulk. Snow wrote that he received five letters claiming that Carmichael never found a penny of treasure and seven letters claiming that he had recovered treasure in amounts estimated between $11,000 and $26,500.

Snow found only a very small portion of the amount of treasure reported on the map. He placed the 1952 value of the treasure remaining after his find at $100,000 and the value of his find at "slightly less than eleven hundred dollars." The present value of the remaining treasure is likely in excess of one million U.S. dollars.

Of course, the treasure isn't the only mystery we are left with. What about the ghost story? Who was the person moving about the pit early that morning when Snow and the Fullerton family approached from the hill above? Was it the ghost of a pirate of bygone days? Who was the poor bloke whose skeleton Snow uncovered?

Edward Low had a flare for the macabre that may have prompted him to play a trick on future generations by placing the human skeleton beside the lake on the eastern end of the island, presumably murdered. The victim had been buried with a fistful of gold and silver coins. Why? If he had been apprehended while trying to steal a bit of Low's loot, surely he wouldn't have been buried with his little cache. Wouldn't Low have retrieved the gold and silver before murdering the thief?

Perhaps Low, in a sadistically playful mood, had a grave dug beside the lake for one of the victims, murdered him, and placed the coins in the corpse's hand before covering it over with soil. Then he prepared several copies of the map that Snow acquired—a "treasure" map pointing to a corpse clutching a few coins—and made sure they would be around for posterity.

And perhaps Dougald Carmichael acquired one of the maps and wasted two trips to Isle Haute in search of the treasure, digging in the wrong places.

Peter Easton and Henry Mainwarring,

Gentleman Pirates

These two drained Newfoundland's resources to pursue their greedy goals.

ichard Whitbourne was an intelligent man. Born into a working-class English family, he spent his entire professional life in Newfoundland, rising through the ranks to become the fishing admiral for the port of St. John's, and he was good at his job. Occasionally, he had to deal with rich and powerful men from Britain, men who could easily use their prestige and influence to make life very difficult for Whitbourne if he didn't comply with their demands. He had to have learned well the skill of dealing with these men, but it still must have been harrowing having to deal with the likes of Peter Easton and Henry Mainwarring.

The year was 1611. Whitbourne sat at the splendid oak table in the great cabin of the *Happy Adventure*, sipping a glass of wine. Opposite him, at the head of the table, the ship's commander, Peter Easton, gestured the steward for more wine. The steward promptly topped up the two partly empty glasses. Easton took a sip and waved the steward a signal to leave the room. Now the two men were alone.

Whitbourne was tired. This was the eleventh week of daily meetings on Easton's big ship. All were secret and the subject never wavered. Day after day, Easton dwelt on his need for men and supplies. He had arrived at Newfoundland that year with ten ships, including his flagship, the *Happy Adventure*, and needed at least an additional five hundred men to carry out his operations—piracy on the high seas. If Whitbourne were to give into any of Easton's requests, he would himself become part of a pirate company. But refusing to co-operate with him was extremely difficult.

Peter Easton was an English gentleman from a family line that had fought in the Crusades and later against the Spanish Armada. He had influential aristocratic connections, the Killigrews of England. The Killigrews were well established with the court, one having been Queen Elizabeth's foreign minister and another the groom of her bedchamber. The Killigrews were the financiers and brokers for many successful pirates, and held Easton with high esteem, regarding him as their prime agent on the high seas. Whitbourne was, by these standards, an utter commoner; Easton, an aristocrat.

Easton was persuasive and patient, explaining over and over that this was not his first visit to Newfoundland. In 1602 he had sailed there as convoy for the Newfoundland fishing fleet, when the English were engaged in hit-and-run warfare at sea with Spain. At that time, those who plundered Spanish ships were considered privateers, not pirates. But in 1603 Queen Elizabeth died, and the new monarch, King James I, made peace with Spain. All letters of marque held by privateers were cancelled. Now what were all these fortune-hunting men of the sea to do for a living? Many, like Easton, saw no alternative but to turn to piracy. What Easton didn't explain to Whitbourne was that although some of the new English pirates plundered only Spanish ships, as if the war were still on, others attacked any ship regardless of nationality—including British vessels. It's quite possible that Easton belonged to the latter group.

Now, as for supplies and crew, what was Easton to do? On his visit of 1602 he legally requisitioned stores, munitions and men. Now he no longer had the right to requisition, all because of the stupid new king who made peace with Spain. Surely, the good fishing admiral must understand.

Whitbourne courageously argued his case. During wartime, the English privateers, preying on enemy commerce, had been an immense help to the war effort—England's navy was in no way powerful enough to protect the Newfoundland fishery by itself. And naturally, the government had had no choice but to provide crewmen and supplies to the privateers as necessary. But because the Spanish were no longer a threat to Newfoundland's fisheries, the fisheries no longer needed privateers' protection, and they simply could not afford to supply Easton with the hundreds of men he was seeking. All the fish available to the English would mean nothing without the men manning the fishing vessels and processing the fish ashore; loss of workers during this time of peace would mean a serious reduction of income to England.

Whether or not Whitbourne's arguments were persuasive, Easton probably did not intend to create a serious reduction in fish production that would decrease England's revenue. He anticipated the returns on his venture to far outweigh the fishery's losses—his sights were set on a few enormously profitable exploits in the West Indies. The Spanish period of conquest of the New World during the sixteenth and seventeenth centuries, following the first voyage of Columbus, was an era in which a vast amount of wealth moved from Mexico, Central America, and South America to Spain. That was when the Spanish began to pilfer archaeological remains of the Maya, Aztec, and Inca empires, snaring gold, silver, pearl, and emerald artefacts. When there was nothing left to plunder, the Spanish went straight to the source, the Indian mines, and billions of dollars worth of gold and silver were smelted into ingots and coins on the spot.

The Spanish convoys usually followed the Gulf Stream up the eastern coast of North America, coming within three or four hundred miles of Newfoundland. Some of the cargoes were immense, evidenced by the amount of treasure that has been recovered from sunken galleons: the *Atocha,* which sank off the coast of Florida in 1622, carried approximately $400 million worth of gold and silver.

So Peter Easton was no fool. As good as the fishing industry was, the advantage of plunder to the south of Newfoundland and Nova Scotia could not be neglected.

Whitbourne may have given into some of Peter Easton's requests, but, given what we know of his character, he more likely stood his ground and continued to say, diplomatically, no. Easton promised him great wealth but there is no evidence that he accepted.

With or without Whitbourne's assistance, however, Peter Easton achieved his goals. He somehow acquired the men, stores, and ammunition he needed. The *Happy Adventure* was a double-decked, three-masted ship of about 350 tons. It required a crew of about 150 men to do battle at full capacity. According to historical sources, Easton took an estimated 1,500 mariners and fishermen out of Newfoundland, and each of his ships was manned by 180 men.

Easton settled his fleet into Harbour Grace, where he careened the ships hulls, made repairs, and added guns and cannons. He either built or occupied a fort, and provided protection to the colony from thieves who would raid their stores of salt and fishing supplies during winter and spring. Public records state that Easton took a hundred cannons from English ships, presumably installing them on his ships at Harbour Grace. He also apparently greatly increased the size of his fleet: records also state that he captured twenty-five French ships, twelve Portuguese ships, and an excellent Flemish vessel.

Fully equipped for conquest in the south, Easton set sail for the West Indies and attacked Puerto Rico, a Spanish colony. He had essentially declared his own war against Spain.

The Spanish were caught completely off guard when what appeared to be a fighting navy sailed over the horizon. They were quite unprepared for an attack by a pirate fleet with the numbers and strength of Captain Easton's. The Spanish had a formidable, well-armed fort called Moro Castle, considered to be impregnable. Other pirates had attempted and failed to take the fort. Easton stormed the fortifications with a ferocity never before experienced by the Spaniards there. He took the fort and loaded his ships with an incredible treasure— Mayan, Aztec, and Inca artefacts. Easton also added another ship to his fleet: the Spanish *San Sebastian*. It was apparently making ready for a shipment to Spain, and was loaded with treasure.

The return voyage was uneventful until Easton reached Harbour Grace. During his absence, a Basque fleet had sailed into the harbour and taken over his fortress. When the Basques saw Easton approaching the harbour, they sailed out to do battle. The Basque fleet, needless to say, made a bad mistake. Every Basque vessel was sunk or captured, and the flagship, the *St. Malo*, was stranded on a tiny island at the entrance to the harbour. When the smoke of battle settled, Easton and his pirate crews dropped anchor and reoccupied their fort.

Easton was now enormously wealthy and prepared to retire. He applied to King James for a pardon. These pardons were frequently purchased, and King James must have been amply rewarded—he issued not one but two pardons. He must have wanted to be doubly certain that Easton would not be prosecuted

But Easton was not quite finished amassing his wealth. In 1614, while still residing with his great fleet in Newfoundland, he learned that a fleet of Spanish treasure ships would soon be setting sail from the Caribbean to Spain via the Azores. This voyage was made annually, when the Spaniards shipped their immense hoards of stolen gold and silver from Central America to the mint in Spain. This was a most valuable tip. It meant that Easton, knowing the date of departure, could reach the Azores before the Spaniards and lie in wait. The Spaniards undoubtedly took a different course through the Azores each time they passed through, so Easton cunningly arranged his ships along a line across the anticipated possible paths of the convoy. The Spanish fleet sailed directly into the ambush. Easton sailed away with the annual loot of Spain.

Now it was truly time for Easton to retire. By current purchasing power, Easton was a multimillionaire at the least and more probably a multibillionaire. In 1615 he cut a deal with the Duke of Savoy and purchased a palace on the Riviera. He adopted the title of Marquis of Savoy, became Master of Ordnance for the Duke of Savoy, and, as they say in fairytale stories, "lived happily ever after."

But this story would not be complete without mention of Henry Mainwarring, another challenge for Richard Whitbourne, and one directly connected to Peter Easton.

Whitbourne must have thought history was repeating itself. Three years after suffering through eleven weeks under the command of the Peter Easton, another gentleman of the piratical profession, Henry Mainwarring, was taking up a great part of his time.

Mainwarring made requests and demands similar to those of Peter Easton. He had arrived in Newfoundland that year of 1614 with eight ships, ostensibly to capture none other than Captain Easton. For that task he demanded additional mariners, carpenters, munitions, and stores.

Mainwarring was several rungs up the ladder of aristocracy from Easton, being a lawyer, scholar, and politician as well as an accomplished soldier and mariner. And he was young to be so accomplished, only twenty-seven years of age. Whitbourne must have struggled hard to deny (if indeed he did deny)

Mainwarring's requisitioning requests. Perhaps even more since his dealings with Peter Easton, he appreciated the peril of clashing with men of such power.

There was, however, a problem with Mainwarring's request to make requisitions: Captain Easton was no longer in or near Newfoundland. Probably, although Whitbourne couldn't have known it, that fact was of little interest to Mainwarring.

In 1610, Mainwarring had been commissioned by the British navy to capture Easton, who had been plundering British merchant ships in the English Channel. But, after he had been outfitted with three sturdy vessels and an abundance of guns, he found out that Easton had sailed off for a foreign voyage—Newfoundland.

Mainwarring found the prospect of abandoning his quest unthinkable. Too much money had been spent on preparations, probably a good amount of his own included. He needed a privateering license, but that was a problem—England wasn't at war at the time. That little matter didn't stop Mainwarring. He applied to the king for letters of marque to plunder Spanish ships. The application was granted on the condition that any preying on Spanish shipping happen outside European waters. The stipulation was apparently not taken seriously; Mainwarring told his captains that they would be capturing the first Spanish ship sighted, inside or outside European waters.

After two years of plundering Spanish ships off the west coast of Africa, Mainwarring set sail for Newfoundland to refit his squadron, which now consisted of eight ships. There he met with Whitbourne, insisting on his great need for help and adamant that he not be refused. He undoubtedly told Whitbourne that he was searching for Captain Easton, which of course would have been easy to prove: he still had his papers of commission.

And those papers gave him the right to requisition experienced sailors, stores, munitions, and tradesmen.

Ironically, Mainwarring spent his time in Newfoundland at Easton's Harbour Grace fort, plundering Portuguese and French ships for everything of value: stores, equipment, munitions and ship's gear. (He must have just missed Easton, who had left for the Azores.) It appears Whitbourne respected Mainwarring's commission; in addition to provisions, equipment, and munitions, he departed with some four hundred men from the Newfoundland fishery.

Spain and France submitted complaints to the king of England regarding Mainwarring's plundering of their ships in Newfoundland, but their pleas for retribution and reimbursements fell on deaf ears. On leaving Newfoundland, Mainwarring returned to Africa and resumed the plundering of Spanish ships. Spain reached the boiling point. Rather than declare war on England, the Spaniards chose to capture Mainwarring and set out after him with a squadron of five warships.

Early in July 1615, the Spanish squadron caught Mainwarring off the coast of Portugal and a vicious battle ensued that ran from dawn to sundown. The Spaniards and Mainwarring exchanged cannon fire, ball for ball, with Mainwarring scoring far more hits. His guns were superior to his opposition and he managed to stay largely out of their reach while relentlessly raking their hulls and decks. Realizing that they could not take Mainwarring, the Spaniards retreated to the shelter of a nearby harbour. Mainwarring ordered his squadron not to follow; his Spanish avengers were now well protected by formidably powerful shore batteries.

Both France and Spain complained to King James, demanding that Mainwarring be declared a highwayman of the sea and placed under arrest—otherwise the peace treaty of the three countries would be considered violated. But rather than apprehend and arrest Mainwarring, King James removed him from piracy by granting him a pardon, an invitation to court, and a Royal Navy commission. Mainwarring accepted.

Back in England and now an honest aristocrat, Henry Mainwarring doled out a very large sum of money, amount unrecorded, to King James. In return, he received a knighthood and the command of Dover Castle, the most vital North Sea fortress. From Dover, he was elected to parliament and rose up through the ranks of the Royal Navy to the position of Vice Admiral.

Now an important and influential gentleman of politics, the court, and the Royal Navy, Mainwarring declared war on piracy. He—of all people!—encouraged the king not to grant pardons for piracy, and influenced his administrators to issue commissions for the capture of pirates. The holder of a commission to capture pirates was offered forty percent of the prize money from the sale of the captured ship's cargo. These worthy recommendations were made in the interest of "safety of the seas"—recommendations made by the pardoned pirate himself, Sir Henry Mainwarring.

So Peter Easton and Henry Mainwarring both met happy endings to their pirating tales. But what of Richard Whitbourne, the stalwart fishing admiral at St. John's, Newfoundland? His patience and skill paid off handsomely: he became a Vice-Admiralty Court judge and was eventually knighted for his many years of faithful and diligent service in Newfoundland.

The Saga of the

Saladin

TRIAL

OF

JONES, HAZELTON, ANDERSON AND TREVASK
ALIAS JOHNSON

FOR

PIRACY AND MURDER

On board barque Saladin,

WITH THE WRITTEN CONFESSIONS OF THE PRISON
Produced in Evidence on the said Trial.

TO WHICH IS ADDED,

PARTICULARS OF THEIR EXECUTION

ON THE 30TH OF JULY

A tale that begins and ends in Nova Scotia, and plunges to the depths of depravity in between.

It is mid-morning on March 30, 2004. I am seated at a writing desk in Lane's Privateer Inn, Liverpool, Nova Scotia. My desk is snuggled up against a small window overlooking Liverpool Harbour. My window provides an excellent view of a long stretch of Main Street, bordering the westerly side of the harbour. I am in Liverpool to do some research on the privateer era of long ago. As I gaze across the water from my vantage point, I give my imagination full range.

I imagine the town as it may have looked a century and a half ago. Has there been a large change? Not much, I speculate; only the colour of the houses, many of which are still standing today. Main Street is not yet paved, people are walking the road, and the occasional horse and buggy makes its way along the travelled lane.

One man on the road stands out from the other pedestrians. He is somewhat advanced in years, but walks with the vigour of one much younger. He has an aura of leadership about him, an ability to make decisions. He is stout, with prominent but not unpleasant features. He is Captain George Fielding. It is the year 1842.

None of this is entirely a figment of my imagination. Captain Fielding belongs to a true saga of piracy and murder on the high seas. And Fielding was not a lone pirate, but the leader of several, who sunk to the depths of depravity.

Captain George Fielding was well known in Liverpool, Nova Scotia; he sailed from there on vessels involved in trade with Newfoundland. Although not well educated, he had a working knowledge of French, Spanish, Portuguese and Dutch, which served him well in his travels. Although not particularly fluent in these languages, he spoke them well enough to ask a basic question and understand a simple reply.

In October 1842, Captain Fielding, in command of the *Vitula*, a fine barque of 460 tons, set sail from Liverpool for Buenos Ayres, Argentina. He was supported by a crew of sixteen men. In addition to the crew, he brought along his son, George, a lad of thirteen or fourteen. Before departing, Captain Fielding—already twice married—tried to persuade a respectable young lady working in a popular Liverpool hotel to marry him, presumably with the intention of taking her along on the voyage. Fortunately for the young lady, the union didn't take place. The young lady's friends stepped in and convinced her to sever her relationship with Fielding.

Fielding reached Buenos Ayres without any problems along the way, but when he found low freights there he continued southerly. He rounded the Horn and sailed up the west coast of South America to Valparaiso, Chile. But when he reached Valparaiso, he found no trade being offered. Desperate not to return home empty handed, he continued northerly to an island of Peru named Chincha, with the plan of smuggling a cargo of guano.

While the *Vitula* was anchored off the island, the Peruvian Government learned of its presence and intention to smuggle. It sent some fifty soldiers to intervene and arrest Captain Fielding and his crew.

The soldiers were landed on the island but given no means of reaching the *Vitula*. It's unclear why no transportation out to the *Vitula* was provided, but the soldiers were most likely ferried out to the island by civilians who did not want to become further involved, or delivered by a Peruvian vessel that preferred not to engage in a battle with the English ship. Regardless of the reason, the Peruvians were undaunted. One bold soldier swam out to the *Vitula*, sliced away the rope attached to her longboat and rowed it back to the island. Now with the longboat to use, as many soldiers as it would hold climbed aboard and pushed off to capture Fielding and his men.

Fielding saw the soldiers approaching in his own longboat but acted too late. He grabbed a large carving knife and tried to cut through the line attached to the ship's anchor to free the vessel and drift it away, but before he could finish the soldiers clambered aboard. Fielding had evidently planned to fight it out—there were large quantities of firearms on the deck—but he was not supported by the crew, who disappeared below deck when the soldiers boarded. Only he and his mate remained to fight and a scuffle ensued in which Fielding was shot in the shoulder.

The Peruvians rounded up the cowering crew from the hold and, after allowing Fielding to change his clothes, disembarked them all into the longboat. Fielding, his son, and the crew were all taken to the island. Fielding was so badly wounded that his fresh change of clothes and even his shoes became drenched with blood before they reached shore. He was ghost white from the injury but never uttered a word of complaint.

The soldiers transferred their captives to a government schooner, took the *Vitula* in tow and both vessels sailed to the harbour of Pisco, about fourteen miles from the island.

When he disembarked, Fielding was too weak from loss of blood to stand or walk. He was placed on a mule and supported by two men. The entire city of Pisco came out to see him drenched in blood and riding a mule.

Captain Fielding received what may be considered good treatment. He was taken to a hospital resembling a church and convent, where he was cared for and his wounds were properly dressed.

After a few days in the hospital Captain Fielding and his crew were placed on board the *Vitula,* and a Peruvian war schooner escorted his vessel to Callao, the seaport of Lima, Peru, about 150 miles north of Pisco. Throughout the voyage, the *Vitula* was taken in tow each night and the crew herded down into the hold and shut in until the next day. Fielding was locked in his cabin under heavy guard and no one was allowed to speak with him.

When the two vessels reached Callao, the crew of the *Vitula* were thrown into prison where they were held for nine days. Fielding, however, was awarded special privileges. He was placed on parole and allowed to go about like any free man.

The *Vitula* was anchored in the harbour of Callao under guard from the fortress. Desperate to have his vessel back, Fielding approached sailors he met on the docks and streets and tried to enlist help to cut his ship free from its moorings late at night and escape. The people with whom he spoke reported his proposal to the authorities. His parole was cancelled and he was put in prison, but even this didn't squelch his ingenuity.

Fielding's son, who had been free during his father's parole, was not arrested and remained to roam about the city and countryside. During a visit, Fielding asked young George to procure him a poncho, which he did. Wrapped in the garment, which disguised him as a native Peruvian, Fielding passed the sentinel on duty and hid for two days and nights beneath a pile of carpenter's shavings and litter. When the opportunity presented itself, he and his son found refuge in the middle of the night on a British ship anchored in the harbour. The vessel took them to back to Valparaiso. In the meantime the *Vitula* was unrigged, condemned by the Peruvians, and sold for the equivalent of $15,000.

At Valparaiso, Fielding tried to find a way home for himself and his son. Captains of the *Jeremiah Garnett* and the *Belfast* declined his requests, and for a while the prospect of gaining passage home looked bleak—but luckily the captain of the *Saladin*, Alexander (Sandy) McKenzie, agreed in a moment of compassion to provide Fielding and his son free passage to London, England.

The *Saladin* was a handsome barque of about 550 tons. Its cabin was splendidly finished with mahogany and other exotic and valuable woods. In keeping with its name, it displayed a beautiful bronze turbaned Turk figurehead. The captain, Sandy McKenzie, had been at sea for about twenty years and had become a competent mariner and ship commander. This was to be his last voyage. When it ended he planned to settle down with his family at Newcastle. There were fourteen aboard, including the captain and Fielding and his son.

Fielding was quick to note that the *Saladin* carried a rich treasure. Its cargo consisted of a huge load of guano, thirteen bars of silver of 150 pounds each, twenty tons of copper, a chest full of dollars, several money letters, and about nine thousand dollars worth of spice.

The *Saladin* set sail on February 8, 1844, and it is probable that Fielding was coveting the ship's rich treasure before McKenzie even pulled anchor. As the vessel sailed south, Fielding sounded out the crew to gain an idea of who he might trust to help him gain control of the ship. Fielding was constantly quarrelling with McKenzie, both men cursing and swearing and shouting at each other. When a verbal fuss ended, Fielding would often discuss the falling out with a crewman, as a way of sounding out the crew. Probably if a sailor said, "Oh, I wouldn't be too hard on old Sandy, he means well," Fielding would count him out as a potential accomplice. On the other hand, should the crewman respond with something to the effect of: "I don't blame you for being mad. If I had me way, I'd cut the old bastard's throat!" Fielding would add him to his list of candidates.

The first man Fielding recruited was George Jones, a sail-maker who acted as steward until crewman John Galloway took the position and Jones returned to the job of repairing sails. Jones was a native of Clare, Ireland. He was of middle height with dark hair and dark complexion. He had blue eyes bordered by heavy lowering eyebrows and wore an expression that suggested suspicion and treachery. He was crippled some years earlier when he fell off a spar and lost a leg. Now he wore a wooden stump and looked all the part of Long John Silver.

Fielding used to speak with Jones about the nature of his quarrels with McKenzie, talked about the amount of treasure on board, and what a great prize it would be for a pirate. Jones implied that Fielding seduced him into compliance with his plan to take over the vessel by suggesting that he had accomplices. Jones claimed that Fielding told him he had spoken with the carpenter, who was second mate, and Jones would be killed if he didn't cooperate. Jones stated that Fielding said, "Now Jones, if you want to save your life, now is the time, I have spoken to the carpenter, and I intend to be master of the ship." Once, in Jones' presence, Fielding made a motion indicating how he would get rid of McKenzie by cutting his throat. After this Jones tried to inform McKenzie of the plot, but was rebuked. "You damned Irishman. I want to hear nothing," McKenzie retorted.

Fielding recruited three more conspirators, all members of the same watch. His plan was to murder the first mate, then the captain, and then the members of the other watch as well as the cook and the crewman who had replaced Jones as steward. They planned to gain control of the *Saladin* and then sail it to the Gulf of St. Lawrence or Newfoundland and hide it in some isolated harbour. Then they would go to the United States, purchase a small vessel, return to the *Saladin* to load up on treasure and sail to a foreign land where they wouldn't be recognized.

The three conspirators in addition to Jones were John Hazelton of Northern Ireland, William Trevaskiss (alias Johnson) of London, and Charles Gustavus Anderson of Uddavalla, Sweden. John Galloway, the new steward who was to be murdered, was a native of Clay Hole, Stranraer, Scotland. The cook, also on the to-be-murdered list was William Carr of North Shields. Both Galloway and Carr became implicated in the atrocities that would take place aboard the *Saladin* and subsequently avoided being murdered.

John Hazelton, suspected to be a native of the United States or Nova Scotia rather than Ireland due to his speech and tone of voice, was an active, well-built twenty-eight-year-old of medium height. He had broad shoulders, a slight stoop, and large, dark eyes. His complexion was also dark, probably from a lot of sun. He had smooth skin and black hair, and long, neatly trimmed whiskers. The expression of his countenance was unquestionably bad. It is recorded that he was "the beau-ideal of a pirate: bold, daring, and reckless."

William Trevaskiss (hereafter Johnson) was a short man of about twenty-three. He had dark blue eyes, a sandy complexion, and a bold, determined countenance that was somewhat forbidding.

Charles Gustavus Anderson, age nineteen, was of medium height. He was well put together, with dark hair, intelligent brown eyes, and a swarthy complexion. He spoke very broken English but he could read and write well in his own language. He had four brothers and five sisters. His father was a man of prominence in his home village back in Sweden—a master shipbuilder.

William Carr, the cook, was a stout and athletic middle-aged man. His face was pockmarked, and he had light blue eyes and a fair complexion. He wore an expression of determination and intelligence and could read and write.

John Galloway, was the same age as Anderson. Being of middle height with a sandy complexion, he was described as "quite a lad." He could read and write and had navigational skills.

Captain McKenzie rounded the Horn without encountering particularly rough waters and by Friday, April 13 was in light winds. The next day, Fielding was ripe for the horrid job to be carried out. He told his accomplices, "It must be done tonight."

As the middle watch ran from midnight to four in the morning, the attack in fact occurred early Sunday. The mate, Thomas Byerby, was at the wheel and not feeling at all well. On deck with Byerby were Fielding and his three partners in crime, John (Jack) Hazelton, William (Bill) Johnson, and Charles Gustavus Anderson.

Hazelton had taken the helm. The mate, with his oil skin coat on and feeling sick, came to him and said, "Jack steer the ship as well as you can, I do not feel well." Then he went forward in his oil skin coat and laid down on the hencoop for a while. He got up and asked Fielding several times to let him go below. Fielding agreed, but first went forward and spoke with the men on the watch; in the meantime, Byerby laid down again on the hencoop and fell asleep.

The carpenter had been working on the deck the day before and his tools—a claw-hammer, maul, adz, broad-axe, among others—were lying in the stern of the long-boat. Armed with the carpenter's tools, Fielding, Johnson, Jones (who had joined the conspirators on deck), and Anderson crept silently to where Byerby lay sleeping. They gathered around the mate and Johnson struck him on the head with the back of a broad-axe. The mate only uttered "oh!" and never spoke another word. Fielding, Johnson and Anderson picked up the body and bundled it overboard. Then Fielding went to the helm and said to Hazelton, "There is one gone."

Some time passed while the murderers decided on their next move. Finally, Anderson and Hazelton went down to the aft-cabin to kill McKenzie but turned back when they heard the captain's brown dog growling or stirring as they approached. The chance of being badly bitten was too great.

They decided that the best way of getting at McKenzie was to lure him up to the deck. They called for the ship's carpenter, also second mate, who slept in the steerage. Johnson, Hazelton and Anderson were stationed around the hatch waiting for their victim. Just before the carpenter reached the deck, Anderson dealt him a hard blow to the head with a hammer. The carpenter was stunned but not killed. Johnson put one hand over his mouth to keep him quiet and seized him by the back of the neck with his other hand while Hazelton and Anderson heisted him up and tumbled him overboard.. He cried "murder" several times after he hit the water—exactly what Fielding wanted him to do. Fielding and Jones cried "A man overboard!" This brought McKenzie scuttling up the companion-way, half undressed, shouting, "Put the helm hard down!" As the captain poked his head above deck, Anderson struck him with a broad-axe—but the blow didn't kill him. The captain caught hold of Anderson and might have subdued him but Jones took hold of the captain along with Anderson. While Anderson and Jones struggled to hold the captain still, Fielding struck him three or four times on the back of his head with an axe. While being struck, McKenzie cried out, "Oh, Captain Fielding! Oh, Captain Fielding, don't!" Fielding said, "Oh, damn you, I will give it to you!" Fielding, Anderson, and Jones then toppled him overboard. During the episode, Fielding's son George stood by, shouting, "Give it to him!"

With three murdered and five left to attend to, Fielding, Anderson, Hazelton, and Johnson took a break and went down to the cabin for a drink of liquor, and Fielding remarked, "The vessel is now our own." Back on deck, Fielding told his son, "I am captain." Young George said to his father, "It was a pity that I had not a blow at Sandy."

For a little while, the murderers discussed what to do next as they stood on the quarter-deck. It was agreed· that Hazelton would take the wheel, Johnson would go forward and call the watch, Jones would lie down in the longboat, and Anderson would lean against the mainmast with his eyes closed, pretending to have dozed off. The men put their plan in action while Fielding concealed himself in the companionway. Young George was behind him with a carving knife, his father having told him to strike any man who might come down.

It was James Allen's turn at the helm so he was the first to come up. Before taking the wheel, Allen said to Hazelton, "Hold on a bit and I will relieve you." Allen was standing on the stern looking out to sea and Anderson snuck up behind him and struck him on the head with an axe or hammer. Fielding, Jones and Hazelton threw him overboard.

After James Allen was disposed of, Jones relieved Hazelton at the helm. Fielding ordered Johnson and Hazelton to haul down the flying-jib. The noise of the jib being lowered brought up Thomas Moffatt and Samuel Collins, the other two men of the watch.

Johnson and Hazelton were seated on the spar by the galley and Moffatt sat down between his two good buddies. As Moffatt turned his head forward, Johnson gave Hazelton a nod and with that they both struck Moffatt on the head with an axe. Hazelton, Johnson, and Jones threw the body overboard. A pool of blood from the blows to Moffatt's head lay on the deck.

Collins had gone into the head, and Anderson, who had pretended to go below, turned and followed him in, striking him with a hammer. Collins dropped overboard.

Fielding took charge of the ship, and all except Hazelton, who was at the helm, went below and into the cabin. Anderson was concerned about what Fielding intended to do about the cook, William Carr, and the steward, young John Galloway. Fielding said, "Leave them to me, I'll give them a dose of poison when we get near land."

In the morning when Carr and Galloway awoke and came on deck they saw that the whole starboard side of the deck was covered with blood. They were told the story of what happened, and that their lives would be spared provided they join the pirate crew. Trevaskiss, Carr and Galloway were appointed to one watch and Hazelton, Jones, and Anderson to another. Carr and Galloway were to sleep in the forecastle and not with the rest of the crew in the cabin.

Down in the cabin, everyone got heavy into the booze.

They bragged about who was the best murderer and laughed and jested with one another. Fielding appointed Hazelton first mate and Johnson second mate. They decided to get rid of all weapons; they didn't trust each other. And rightly so: given the atrocities they had all committed, and the value of the ship and its treasure, no one could be counted on. They threw overboard all of the carpenter's tools left in the longboat. All firearms and cutlasses were similarly disposed of, except for one cutlass and a fowling piece that might be necessary to pick up extra food. Then Fielding made everyone swear on a bible that they would be brotherly.

After breakfast on the day of the slaughter, they ransacked the cabin. They broke open bags and boxes of letters looking for money, cutting the postage off the letters. They smashed open desks, trunks, and drawers in search of money, and distributed the clothes of the murdered men between themselves. The rampage went on until evening.

Later that night Fielding went to Galloway, who was in the cabin alone, and proposed that Galloway and he kill everyone remaining except his son, Anderson, and Hazelton. Galloway refused. Fielding then made a similar proposal to Anderson, who told all the crew what Fielding had in mind.

On the evening of Monday, April 16, Hazelton and Johnson searched the ship and found two pistols hidden under the cabin's table. A further search turned up a carving knife that had been missing since Sunday morning and two bottles of brandy which were suspected of containing poison. They also found a bottle of poison in Fielding's locker.

Hazelton and Johnson accused Fielding of concealing the pistols for the purpose of killing off most of the crew. Johnson and Carr laid hold of Fielding, tied his hands and feet, laid him down on the floor, and kept watch over him all night until the following morning. All during this time, Fielding's son was up on deck with the crew. In the morning, Johnson and Hazelton untied Fielding's feet, led him up onto the deck, and then retied his feet. He was constrained in this way for some time while he screamed and shouted to such an extent that

Johnson gagged him on the crew's request.

After breakfast, Jones and Carr heaved him overboard. Galloway was asked to help throw Fielding over the side but he refused. He was then told that if he would not assist in pitching Fielding into the sea, he should at least touch him. This Galloway did.

After Fielding was overboard, the rest of the crew persuaded Carr and Galloway to take hold of Fielding's son and drag him to the larboard gangway. The boy kicked and screamed and clung to Galloway while hanging over the ship's side. The crew shouted, "shake him off!" While clutching, the boy ripped off some of Galloway's clothes. Galloway pushed and shoved and managed to free himself from the boy and let him fall to the water below.

Everybody agreed that Galloway would take charge of the vessel as navigator because he was the best scholar. They agreed on a plan: they would sail up to Cape Breton Island or Newfoundland, scuttle the ship, and take the longboat up the Gulf of St. Lawrence.

To lighten the vessel, they spent one full morning heaving nearly eight tons of copper overboard. Anxious to conceal the identity of the ship, they nailed a board over the name of the vessel on the stern, and painted the bronze figurehead of a Turk on the bow white.

About two days after Fielding's murder, the specie (coins) were divided among the crew. Each pirate took his share and put it in a stocking or bag; all these were deposited in a chest in the cabin. Everyone on board took an oath never to tell of the murders that took place upon the *Saladin* nor divulge details concerning the concealment of the money.

Beginning the day of the first murders aboard the *Saladin*, the crew got heavily into liquor, of which there was an abundant supply; after Fielding and his son were murdered, a portion of the crew was drunk every day. It is not unreasonable to presume that almost every pirate on the vessel was either drunk or suffering from a hang-over every day of the week. This condition probably greatly contributed to an event that the country folk of the far eastern shore of Nova Scotia have long remembered and recounted.

On the morning of May 22, 1844, the *Saladin* crashed hard up on the shore of Harbour Island, Nova Scotia, on a point of land that now bears the name of the vessel. Harbour Island is situated off the mouth of Country Harbour, about a hundred miles east of the harbour mouth of Halifax.

Captain Cunningham, of the schooner *Billow*, was anchored in a nearby harbour when he was informed that a large barque had run ashore on Harbour Island. He wasted no time getting out to the stranded ship, despite very rough weather.

When Cunningham came in sight of the wreck, a man was standing on the bowsprit, calling for assistance with a speaking trumpet. On reaching the vessel, Cunningham was shocked to learn that the wrecked barque was the *Saladin* of Newcastle, on a voyage from Valparaiso to London, England.

On boarding the *Saladin*, Cunningham was told that the captain had died about seven or eight weeks earlier; the first officer had died three days later; and the remaining men had fallen and either been drowned or killed in the accidents.

Cunningham found almost everything on board to be in confusion and disorder. Valuable property of every description was scattered about and bunched together in the utmost disorder: every variety of men's clothing; nautical instruments such as quadrants, chronometers and a very valuable sextant that had obviously been disassembled to satisfy some sailor's curiosity; ships' letters, bills of exchange, and indentures; and a chest of dollars filled almost to overflow.

Examining the ship's log, Cunningham noted that the *Saladin* had left Valparaiso on February 8 and the last entry in the log was April 14. He found clothing made for a young boy. Something was very wrong; Cunningham's suspicions grew. He sent a letter to the nearest magistrate and soon the pirates were arrested and brought to Halifax to stand trial for piracy. They were thrown into the prison on Melville Island on the Northwest Arm, where the Armdale Yacht Club is now situated. (The old prison still stands on the water's edge and has been used for a great number of years by yacht club members to store their boating equipment.)

The legal process was easy for the judge, lawyers and jury. Galloway and Carr called for a lawyer and gave honest accounts of their crimes and those of their shipmates. Confessions from Jones, Johnson (Trevaskiss), Hazelton, and Anderson subsequently followed. The pleas were changed from piracy to murder for all the prisoners.

Following the trial of Jones, Johnson, Hazelton, and Anderson, the jury retired briefly, returning after about fifteen minutes with a verdict of "guilty." The convicted men were sentenced to be hanged.

However, Galloway and Carr, charged with the murder of Captain Fielding and his son, were lucky. The jury took about two hours to agree on a verdict of "not guilty." The jury based its decision on a plea that the two men were forced to commit the murders by the other crewmen. It may be presumed that the jury considered that they had acted in self defense.

The four condemned men were executed on what is now known as the South Common on Tuesday, July 30, 1844. The gallows was erected on a hill in the rear of a small Catholic cemetery. A company of the 52nd Regiment arrived early on the hanging grounds and made a circle around the gallows to keep the spectators at a respectable distance.

The prisoners were taken to their executions in two horse-drawn carriages, preceded by the sheriff in a gig. The procession was heavily guarded by a group of soldiers with bayonets. The condemned men arrived at about 10 A.M. Three Catholic priests attended to the two Irishmen, Jones and Hazelton, and an Anglican clergyman attended to Johnson and the Swede, Anderson.

The execution was a spectacular event and thousands of Halifax citizens turned out to see the morbid undertaking. One man from Lunenburg County was so enthralled by the tale of degenerate piracy, which had begun in his very own province, that he walked fifty miles to view the hanging.

The Suspicious Story of the
𝕸𝖆𝖗𝖞 𝕮𝖊𝖑𝖊𝖘𝖙𝖊

Two Nova

Scotian ships

at the centre

of a

high-seas

mystery.

y pure coincidence, two brigantines built in Nova Scotia—the *Mary Celeste* and the slightly larger *Dei Gratia* ("by grace of God")—sailed across the North Atlantic eight days apart in November 1872. Both vessels departed from New York and both were bound for Genoa, Italy. Both ships carried dangerous cargoes: the *Mary Celeste* was loaded down with 1,701 barrels of industrial alcohol and the *Dei Gratia's* hold was filled with barrels of petroleum.

Captain Benjamin S. Briggs, age thirty-seven, was commander of the *Mary Celeste*. He was a shipmaster of substantial financial stature, an owner of a third of the vessel, and a descendant of other sea captains. Born at Wareham, Massachusetts, he went to sea at an early age—before purchasing his share in the *Mary Celeste*, he had commanded four other ships. He was a mariner of substantial experience, especially for his young age. The United States' consul once remarked, "Briggs I had known for many years, and he always bore a good character as a Christian and as an intelligent and active shipmate."

The *Mary Celeste* was less than twelve years old, weighed 282 tons, and was about a hundred feet long by twenty-three feet wide. It was large enough to weather the worst of storms, and a captain with six mariners could sail it anywhere.

Mary Celeste was not the vessel's original name. Designed by Gideon Bigelow of Canning, Nova Scotia, and built at Spencer Island (a little village on the northern shore of the Minas Channel) by Joshua Dewis and his assistants, the ship was first called *Amazon*. The ship was completed in 1861, and then went aground near Glace Bay, Cape Breton Island, in November 1867. It was sold, refloated, and then sold again at an auction in New York for $1750. A shrewd shipmaster, Richard Haines avoided American import taxes by having a customs broker acquire American registration for the ship, and then renamed it *Mary Celeste*. Haines sailed the renamed brigantine himself for about a year, but when he encountered some kind of financial problem, the ship was seized at New York and sold against his debt. The new owner was a former Nova Scotia sea captain, James H. Winchester. He spent $11,500 repairing and enlarging the ship, bringing up its tonnage to 282 from 198.42. It was after this work was done that he sold a third of the ship to Captain Briggs.

There were ten people aboard the *Mary Celeste* when it pulled anchor in November 1872 for the voyage from New York to Genoa: Captain Briggs, his wife Sarah, and their baby girl, Sophy; first mate Albert Richardson, of Maine, who had sailed with Briggs before; second mate Andrew Gilling, of Denmark; two brothers, Volkert and Boz Lorenzen, of the Frisian Islands, Germany; Arian Martens and Gottlieb Gottschalk, also of Germany; and the cook and steward,

Edward Head, from New York. With the exception of Arian Martens, who was two years younger than Captain Briggs, the crewmen were in their twenties. All were known in their home communities to be respectable, honest and reliable gentlemen. Briggs and his wife also had a boy, Arthur, age seven. He was left behind with his grandmother Briggs at Marion, Massachusetts, to attend school. In addition to the ten people, there was one other of God's creatures on board: a cat, to keep the rat population in check.

The *Mary Celeste* set sail on the morning of November 7, 1872, after a two-day delay in which it waited in the harbour for improved weather conditions. November and December can be rough out on the North Atlantic, and there had been a strong headwind outside the harbour, but at last the wind favoured good sailing, at least temporarily.

The *Dei Gratia* was being loaded at Hoboken, in the port of New York, on November 7 when the *Mary Celeste* finally got underway. Captain David Morehouse and his first mate, Oliver Deveau, were both Nova Scotians and capable seamen. Morehouse was from Digby and belonged to a well-recognized seafaring family; Deveau, an Acadian, was from Saint Mary's Bay.

The *Dei Gratia* set sail eight days after the *Mary Celeste* and fought high winds and rough seas on most of the voyage, arriving at Gibraltar on December 12. Here, Captain Morehouse was required to stop and go through some red tape—receive orders, as was the Mediterranean trade procedure—before proceeding to Genoa.

Morehouse told the authorities that he had another ship, a similar but somewhat smaller brigantine, scheduled to arrive shortly. It was a derelict that he had salvaged during his transatlantic voyage.

It was a vessel from New York, named the *Mary Celeste*.

The following day, Friday, December 13, the *Mary Celeste* arrived, sailed by three men of the *Dei Gratia*, the first mate, Oliver Deveau, and two seamen. There was not another soul on board. The Marshal of the Vice-Admiralty court at Gibraltar immediately took the *Mary Celeste* into custody. A hearing began five days later on Wednesday, December 18, just a week before Christmas.

Captain Morehouse recounted one of the strangest events involving ships on the high seas. The Vice-Admiralty Judge and others in attendance listened in awe as the story was told.

The Azores Islands, about a thousand miles off the coast of Portugal, is on the sea route from New York to Gibraltar. Captain Morehouse had sailed past the north of the islands and was headed for Gibraltar when a brigantine much like the *Dei Gratia* was spotted. It was early afternoon on December 4. One of the seamen was at the wheel and Captain Morehouse stood nearby. They sailed closer and Morehouse took a look with his spy-glass. He noticed that the vessel "was under very short canvas, steering very wild, and evidently in distress." He summoned the first mate, Deveau, to take a look. Deveau came up on deck and estimated the vessel to be about four or five miles from them. Morehouse proposed that they speak to the vessel and instructed the crew to put up more sail and draw nearer. On reaching a close—but still safe—distance from the brigantine, Morehouse had the horn brought up from the cabin and hailed the ship. He waited for a response. There was none. He hailed again and still there was no answer. Something was very wrong.

Morehouse and Deveau noticed that the vessel's sails were in a state of disorder—some were furled, others hung loose, and two had obviously been torn off the yards, as all that remained were rags of canvas. There were no boats on board or in tow. No one was at the wheel. The deck was empty.

At three o'clock that afternoon, Deveau and two sailors rowed over to the ship and noted *Mary Celeste, New York*, painted on the stern. Deveau shouted, "Permission to come aboard," but there was no reply so they boarded without invitation. Once on deck they called out for an answer but again there was no reply. Then they searched the vessel and were shocked to discover that there was not a soul aboard. Even the ship's cat was missing.

Although the cabin windows were covered from outside for protection from rough weather, openings that should have been closed and well battened were not. The cabin skylight, the galley doors, the companionway, and the forecastle were all open. So were the hatches of the forehold and lazarette, their covers cast aside on the deck. Seawater splashed around inside the cabin and galley and three and a half feet of water sloshed among the barrels of alcohol down in the hold, although these remained in place and well secured. The bilge pumps were in good working order. There was no visible damage to the hull. There was, however, evidence that large waves had washed over the deck. Freshwater casks had been displaced, the binnacle was broken, and the compass was smashed. The galley stove was pushed out of place by waves that had surged through the open door and there was no fire inside. The stove was cold. All cooking utensils hung on hooks in their proper locations.

There were indications of a hasty departure. The bedding in the berth of the Captain's cabin was unmade. There was no food on the table, none cooked in the galley, and the cutlery was properly placed in the pantry, knives and forks and spoons each in their appropriate slots. The captain's chronometer and sextant were missing; however, most of his charts and books had been left behind. Most of the captain's clothing and those of his wife and baby girl remained in the cabin. A child's doll also remained. Sarah Briggs had brought a sewing machine on board; it was still in its place. The storeroom was well stocked with provisions including an ample supply of fresh water. The seamen's possessions in the forecastle remained. Their sea chests contained valuables, and a British five-pound banknote lay visible in one. And most astonishingly, their tobacco pouches and pipes remained behind. It is incomprehensible that a sailor would not take his pipe and tobacco with him when abandoning ship.

The islands of the Azores run in southeast toward Europe and stretch about four hundred miles. The farthest island to the west is Santa Cruz, and one of the most easterly is Santa Maria, known to sailors as Saint Mary's Island.

Daily entries were made in the *Mary Celeste*'s logbook up to Sunday, November 24. An entry made that day in the working log, a slate kept by the mate, read, "At 5 o'clock made the island of St. Mary's bearing E.S.E. At 8, Eastern point bore S.S.W. 6 miles distant."

The "Eastern" point referred to is the easterly finger of Santa Maria Island. It is known as Castello Point and is the last landmark en route to Gibraltar. The *Mary Celeste* had apparently sailed along the north side of the island and a departure bearing would have been taken on Castello Point for the last leg of the voyage to Gibraltar. From a determination of latitude and longitude taken on board the *Dei Gratia* on December 4, it was determined that the *Mary Celeste* had drifted to a point about eight hundred miles away from Santa Maria before she was overtaken ten days later.

When Deveau returned to his ship and reported the mysterious situation on board the *Mary Celeste*, Captain Morehouse made a serious decision. It was estimated that they still had six hundred miles to go to reach Gibraltar, undoubtedly in rough seas. What would he do with the *Mary Celeste*? It was carrying a very valuable cargo. If they could safely bring the ship into port there would be a lot of salvage money for the owner, J. H. Winchester, and a good amount for Morehouse, Deveau, and members of the crew. To bring the *Mary Celeste* to Gibraltar, it would be necessary to divide his small crew. What if they ran into a bad storm? There might not be sufficient hands on either vessel and both could be lost. Still, the lure of big money won. Morehouse and Deveau agreed to run the risk.

Deveau and two seamen took on the task of sailing the *Mary Celeste* to port. They took the *Dei Gratia*'s small boat and went over to the derelict with cooked provisions and navigational instruments. It was only a half hour before sundown when they boarded the *Mary Celeste* to begin the voyage. There was a lot to be done in a short time so they went to work immediately. They replaced the hatches, pumped out the hold, and mopped up the water in the cabin and galley. They fashioned a makeshift foresail, set the remaining sails, and within a few hours struck out behind the *Dei Gratia*.

They didn't encounter any unusually bad weather and the two brigantines managed to sail together for six days, sighting Cape Spartel on the afternoon of Wednesday, December 11. But a vicious storm with high winds and rain developed that day and the two ships were separated during the night. Captain Morehouse struggled into Gibraltar the next day but the *Mary Celeste* was nowhere in sight. Luckily, Deveau sailed the *Mary Celeste* into Gibraltar the next day. The vessel had been blown through the Gibraltar Strait to Ceuta on the African coast; from there Deveau crossed over to the Spanish side and worked his way back to Gibraltar Bay. Of the experience, Deveau wrote his wife, "My men were all done out when I got in here, and I think it will be a week before I can do anything, for I never was so tired in my life. I can hardly tell what I am made of, but I do not care as long as I got in safe. I shall be well paid, for the *Mary Celeste* . . . was loaded with alcohol . . . and her cargo is worth eighty thousand dollars besides the vessel." Deveau went on to write that he didn't know how the settlement would be made, that Captain Morehouse would probably have to stop while he continued on the voyage with the *Dei Gratia*.

Neither the Court nor the general public believed much of Captain Morehouse's story. It just seemed too incredible to be true. Had Morehouse and his mate made up this wild tale, so wild that there would be no loose ends to investigate? Had they made the story so cut-and-dry and crazy that there would be no possibility of conflicting statements? Was the story based on the theory that no one would ever contrive anything so far fetched, and therefore no one would suspect them of lying?

The hearing dragged on and on, one attorney in particular—Frederick S. Flood, "Advocate and Proctor for her Majesty the Queen"—being particularly skeptical of the evidence given. He suspected foul play.

Captain Briggs had picked up an antique sword as a souvenir on one of his visits to Italy and had stowed it under his berth. Flood inspected the ship and found rust-coloured spots on the deck and on the sword. He declared them bloodstains. The spots were examined by a chemist who decided that they were not, but science was not as precise then as it is now. Was his analysis accurate?

After ten days, Captain Morehouse sent first mate Deveau and the *Dei Gratia* on to Genoa to make the petroleum delivery. This move on Morehouse's part was rather foolish, as it furthered Flood's suspicion of criminal activity. Although ten days had passed since the court case began, it commenced only a week before Christmas, and it was probably not until after New Year's day that proceedings got seriously under way. It was a poor time to send Deveau off on the *Dei Gratia*. Judge Cochrane apparently also became suspicious of foul play upon Deveau's departure, for he remarked, "It appears very strange why the captain of the *Dei Gratia*, who knows very little or nothing to help the investigation should remain here, whilst the first mate and crew who boarded the *Celeste* and brought her here should have been allowed to go away as they have done." When Deveau reached Genoa, he was ordered to leave the *Dei Gratia* in command of the second mate and return to the hearing at Gibraltar.

When he was questioned about the presumed blood stains on the deck and sword, Deveau testified that he had not noticed any traces of blood on the deck. As for the sword, he said, "I found that sword under the Captain's berth. There was nothing remarkable on it. I do not think there is anything remarkable about it now. It seems rusty." Deveau told the court that it had not occurred to him that there had been "any act of violence." He said that there had been nothing to induce him "to believe or to show that there had been any violence."

Captain Morehouse gave the court the following theory: Fumes of escaped alcohol suddenly entered the fore and aft living quarters of the *Mary Celeste*. (Alcohol fumes in a confined space are extremely dangerous and can cause an explosion if exposed to even a tiny spark or flame.) Everyone on board caught smell of alcohol at the same time. Captain Briggs ordered the doors, cabin skylight, and hatch covers opened. The danger was probably soon over, but the sailors panicked and insisted on escaping in the ship's boat. Captain Briggs had no alternative but to join them. He took along his wife and baby and hoped to reason with his men after they were out on the water and not far from the ship. After the boat was lowered, they all climbed aboard, even the cat. As a precaution, should they not be able to get back to the ship, Briggs took along his sextant and chronometer. Briggs's plan was to persuade his men not to get too far away from the ship and to wait to see if anything at all happened, so he had secured a long tow-rope and let the *Mary Celeste* pull them along at a safe distance astern. If the vessel didn't explode within a reasonable length of time they would reboard and continue on with the voyage. But the wind sprang up to gale force and the ship bounded forward, snapping the tow-rope free of the ship. No amount of hard rowing allowed them to catch up to the *Mary Celeste* as it raced away. The helpless souls perished in the cold stormy sea when their boat swamped or capsized.

Flood, in a report to the British Board of Trade, gave his own theory about what happened. He wrote:

"My own theory or guess is that the crew got at the alcohol, and in the fury of drunkenness murdered the Master, his wife and child and the chief mate; that they then damaged the bows of the vessel with a view to giving it the appearance of having struck on the rocks, or suffered a collision, so as to induce the master of any vessel which might pick them up, if they saw her at some distance, to think her not worth attempting to save; and that they did, some time between the 25th November and 5th December, escape on board some vessel bound for some North or South American port or the West Indies."

As the hearing dragged on, the owner of the *Dei Gratia*, J. H. Winchester, arrived from New York with George Blatchford of Massachusetts, who was to be the new captain of the *Mary Celeste*. Winchester was eager to get the brigantine and its cargo off to Genoa, but ran into problems with Flood. Flood was insinuating in court (and in letters to the British Board of Trade) that someone had bribed the seamen of the *Mary Celeste* to murder its captain and mates and leave it floating around at a specified point near the Azores, where it would be "discovered" by salvagers. Winchester acted highly insulted, as if he were being accused, and left the courtroom in a rage. He returned to New York, leaving a Gibraltar lawyer to fight the case to the end and leaving Captain Blatchford behind to take command of the *Mary Celeste* when it was released.

The Court failed to find Captain Morehouse, his mate Deveau, or any of the crew of the *Dei Gratia* guilty of foul play and, on March 10, 1873, after spending ten days refitting sails and running rigging, Captain Blatchford sailed the *Mary Celeste* for Genoa.

Only about $8,300 in United States currency, which represented a tiny portion of the *Mary Celeste's* total worth, was awarded to the salvagers. The whole affair was tainted with a suspicion of piracy and murder; few were able to believe that ten people could simply vanish from a sound ship out in the middle of the North Atlantic.

Piracy and Murder on the
$\mathfrak{Zero}$

The tale

of the

last pirate

hanged in

Canada.

The story of piracy and murder to unfold here took place off the coast of Nova Scotia, but it sprouted from a seed planted in Jamaica in or before the year 1865. An experienced white mariner, John C. Douglas, and a black cook, Henry Dowsey (some accounts spell his name Dowcey or Downey), became acquainted. Most of the details and events related in this story are from a testimony given by Henry Dowsey.

One day in 1865 the mail steamer *Montezuma* stopped at Jamaica en route to New York. Douglas hired on to work off his passage to the Big Apple, and Dowsey signed on as a member of the crew. During the voyage, the two men became close friends and decided to sail together after they reached New York.

When the *Montezuma* reached the port of New York, Dowsey slipped off the steamer and Douglas smuggled Dowsey's sea-chest ashore. The two men took separate boarding houses.

Soon after arriving at New York, Douglas found a position as mate on the brigantine *Zero*, owned by J. W. Whitney and Company of New York. The captain, Colin C. Benson, a resident of Grand Manan, New Brunswick, was a small man of about forty years of age. Light and thin, with a broken leg, he was five feet five inches tall and weighed about 125 pounds. He was in the process of taking on a crew to take on a cargo of coal at Cow Bay, Cape Breton Island, and deliver it to a port in the United States.

Douglas took Dowsey on board one morning and recommended him to the captain, saying that Dowsey was a boatswain who had sailed with him for some time. The captain refused to hire Dowsey in any capacity, saying that he preferred to have an entirely white crew. Dowsey went back to his boarding house, and Captain Benson completed his hiring, which, despite the fact that he preferred a white crew, included a dark-complexioned cook. The cook didn't suit Captain Benson, and he was fired; unknown to Captain Benson, Douglas went to see Dowsey at his boarding house and told him he could be cook on the *Zero*.

When Captain Benson set sail for Cow Bay, his crew consisted of John Douglas, mate; Henry Dowsey, cook; three Germans; one Englishman; and a fifteen-year-old cabin boy, Frank Howard Stockwell. The son of a Massachusetts Baptist minister, Stockwell had defied his parents, run away from home, and signed on the *Zero* in New York. Although Captain Benson was probably surprised to discover that Henry Dowsey, whom he had earlier refused to hire, was his new cook, he merely went to Dowsey and said, "So you are going with us after all," and let the matter stand.

Dowsey was encouraged to sail with Douglas in view of a brighter future. Captain Benson had initially offered wages to

Douglas that he found unacceptable but the two men reached a settlement. Captain Benson told Douglas that he was part owner of a brig of Sydney, Cape Breton, and would place him in command of the vessel when they reached Cow Bay. Douglas then told Dowsey that he could go with him when he gained command of the brig and they would "always be together."

Dowsey noted that Captain Benson didn't seem to like Douglas. When they reached Cow Bay, Benson went directly to Sydney, where the brig was docked, and gave orders for the ship to be sailed to New York in command of its present captain. When Benson returned to Cow Bay, he told Douglas that the brig had left for New York before he arrived in Sydney, so command of the ship could not be changed. Understandably, Douglas was angry over this and the two men were on bad terms with each other all the time the coal was being loaded.

Before the *Zero* set sail to return to New York, the three German seamen deserted, and the Englishman had to be discharged as he had become sick. Captain Benson blamed Douglas for the desertion of the Germans, and Douglas in turn became angrier than ever with the captain.

After the coal was loaded, Captain Benson pulled away from the dock, anchored off some distance out in the water, and went ashore late at night. Stockwell heard the captain saying that he had made this manoeuvre because he understood that his mate was trying to induce his cook and cabin boy to run away. When Captain Benson came back to the ship, Stockwell told Douglas what the captain had said. No words were exchanged between the mate and captain that night, and the next morning the captain left immediately for Sydney to recruit additional crew, leaving Stockwell in charge of the vessel.

After the captain left the ship, Douglas told Dowsey what the cabin boy had told him the night before. He said that since the captain had such a rotten opinion of him, he had a good mind to run off with the brig. Then he asked Dowsey if he would go with him on the *Zero* to Newfoundland. Dowsey refused. Douglas told Dowsey that he needn't be afraid as he could go ashore and hire on more men. Dowsey replied that he would have trouble pulling off the heist because there were too many ships in the harbour. Douglas said that he would wait until that night when it was dark, pull anchor, and sail out of the harbour without a problem. Douglas pressed his companion hard to consent to the plot but without success. Then he made another proposal. If he didn't run off with the *Zero*, he would steal its boat and instead go to some other place, perhaps Prince Edward Island. He asked Dowsey and Stockwell to join him. They agreed.

That afternoon they prepared to leave with the boat. Stockwell was sent to climb through the window of the locked captain's cabin and get a chart, the captain's ammunition and revolver, and any money that might be there. Although Stockwell could find neither money nor revolver, he did snap up a chart and deliver it to Douglas, who tucked it away among his navigational instruments. Douglas was now about ready to push off, but first he ordered Dowsey and the boy to bring on two barrels of flour and a barrel of pork to sell ashore to raise some money for the voyage. By seven in the evening they had the boat's mast up and were ready to set sail but ran into a problem: the boat was overloaded. They decided to take only loose meat, not in barrels. Now all they had left to do was gather up and bring aboard their clothes, which they were in the process of doing when Captain Benson came alongside! He had recruits with him: two Germans, Charles Marlbey and William (Bill) Lambrach. He and the Germans boarded the *Zero*, saw the boat on the opposite side of the vessel, and went over to take a look.

"What's going on here?" Benson yelled. "What boat is that?"

"It's our boat," Douglas replied.

"What is she doing with a mast in her?" Benson asked.

Douglas was quite straightforward with an explanation. He indignantly responded, as if he were doing nothing wrong: "You have been speaking badly about me to other captains, and you accused me of trying to run away from the vessel with the steward [the cook] and boy, and besides you disappointed me of the promise you made to me of giving me command of a brig in Sydney. Therefore I have made up my mind to go away, and I was going away when you came on board."

Benson said, "Well, that is a very hard job, too; I left you in charge of my vessel, and just now you were going away, and would leave her all alone."

Douglas told Benson that he would have "secured" the vessel and Benson said he didn't believe him. And with that, Benson ordered Dowsey to get everything out of the boat. When Dowsey finished, Benson had the crew hoist the boat in and gave orders to pull the anchor and get the trip underway.

While Benson gave his orders, Douglas protested and refused to obey. He tried to persuade the crew to ignore the captain but they refused and went about the work of preparing the vessel for departure.

Benson then spoke with Douglas, who told him there were not enough hands on board and that he would not consent to go to sea with such a small crew. A discussion ensued in which the captain explained that he had often gone to sea with "just as few hands," and there was no reason why they shouldn't on this voyage. Benson was persistent in his argument and tried very hard to persuade his mate to change his mind and get on with the work. Seeing that the crewmen were not going to side in with him, Douglas finally gave in.

That night, Thursday, September 7, 1865, the *Zero* set sail from Cow Bay.

Benson and Douglas became increasingly bitter towards each other, and Douglas schemed with the cabin boy on ways to take the ship or its boat. The cook, Dowsey, said in a statement that "everything was, after this, upside down with the mate and the captain. The mate did not eat a meal with the captain until Saturday at dinner time. In the meantime the mate and the boy were plotting and the boy told the mate everything that he heard the captain say about him."

Dowsey told of trouble that began on the night of departure:

Thursday night, the watches were divided, the captain took the two Germans, and gave the boy to the mate. Then the mate refused to take the helm, and the boy had to steer the vessel. This caused a great confusion between the mate and the captain, because the boy was not able to steer the vessel properly. The mate said he didn't ship [sign on] to steer, and the captain said that he might just as well take the wheel himself, as he was short of men. The mate still refused. During the night watch on Friday the boy got the vessel on a wrong tack; the captain was asleep then, and this waked him up; he came up on deck, took the wheel from the boy, got the vessel all right again, and was forced to stop [stay] up all night to keep his own watch, and the mate's too, because the mate had refused to steer on this as on the previous night. On Saturday, after dinner, the captain called one of the Germans aft, and he wanted him to sign the articles. The German refused doing it, as he said the captain had promised to give him and the other German $25 [for] the run instead of, as the captain said, $25 [for] the month.

Then the captain called the other German, and he also refused to sign the articles. The captain said if they didn't sign that day, they would sign on Monday. He said this as if he intended to make them do it by force, or by coaxing, or some other way. The Germans then went away, and the captain called the boy, and told him if he should see anything going wrong between the mate and the men forward, that he was to acquaint him, and he would use his revolver, if necessary. The boy came forward and told the mate all this. Then the mate went to the Germans, and told them that they would be foolish if they signed the papers. After this the captain called the mate aft, and spoke to him about going away with the boat, and he and the captain then had an awful row. The captain threatened that he would put the mate in jail when he got to port and the boy and me as well.

This took place on Saturday afternoon, about one o'clock. No blows were struck between the captain and the mate when they had the quarrel. The captain afterwards went below, and turned in. It was the mate's watch on deck with Charlie, the German. After the captain had turned in, the mate came forward and called me out of the galley. I was not aware of the row in the cabin until the mate told me of it, and what I have said about the above, the mate told me. The mate also said to me he was sorry that he had not his own revolvers on deck with him when the captain came on board on Thursday night—that he would have shot him off the ship's rail where he was standing, and have gone away with the boat after all.

Douglas told Dowsey on that Saturday afternoon of September 9 that it had always been his intention to do the captain a "private injury," and that he was going to perform it before they got to port with the load of coal. He told Dowsey that if he could get the Germans to throw the captain overboard, he would alter the ship's papers, sail the ship to the West Indies, sell the cargo, sail on down to the Spanish Main, sell the ship, and divide all proceeds among the crew. He said that he didn't want to kill the captain himself but would like to have the Germans do it.

Having laid out his plan, Douglas told Dowsey to approach the Germans and ask them if they would perform the nasty deed on the captain. Dowsey didn't refuse, but he expressed concern that Douglas wouldn't be able to alter the ship's papers. Douglas assured him that it would not be a problem. "I can alter any ship's papers," he said.

One of the Germans, Charles Marlbey, was working nearby when Douglas and Dowsey were talking. Dowsey asked him if he had overheard what they were discussing and he said he hadn't because they were talking too fast—he could speak

English but needed to hear the words pronounced slowly. Dowsey told Marlbey what the mate was planning. Marlbey told Dowsey he "did not know what to say." He told Dowsey to speak with the other German, Bill Lambrach—he would go along with whatever Lambrach said.

At four o'clock that afternoon, Douglas asked Dowsey if he had spoken with the Germans about the mutinous plan; Dowsey told him that Marlbey didn't seem to like it. Douglas told Dowsey to speak with the Germans again, so at suppertime Dowsey went to the forecastle and found the two Germans engaged in a lively conversation. Wondering what they might have been talking about, Dowsey approached Marlbey and inquired. Marlbey told him that he had been telling Lambrach about the matter and both disapproved. Murder was a serious offence, and they both feared being thrown into prison when they reached the West Indies.

After supper on that Saturday evening, Douglas asked Dowsey once again what the Germans thought of the plan. Dowsey replied that "they did not seem to agree with it." Douglas said, "Never mind, they will agree to it another time, likely."

A short time later Lambrach crossed paths with Dowsey in the forecastle and asked him why he didn't push the captain overboard himself. Dowsey got the impression that Lambrach was willing to join in the murderous scheming but had been discouraged by Charles's refusal and wanted Dowsey to commit the crime. Dowsey told Lambrach that if he had as good a chance as Lambrach had, he would. Lambrach then suggested they draw lots. The loser had to dispose of the captain. Dowsey didn't like that proposal and rejected it.

About eight o'clock that night, Douglas went to the galley and spoke with Dowsey. He asked, "Are we going to do it, or not?" Dowsey said that since the Germans had refused he didn't want anything to do with it. Douglas tried to persuade Dowsey to take the matter in his own hands, but Dowsey was reluctant to say he would. No more was said about the matter until the following morning, Sunday, September 10.

Near the break of day Captain Benson was in his berth, having taken a turn at the wheel beginning at four o'clock that morning. Douglas and the cabin boy, Stockwell, were in the galley with Dowsey as he cooked breakfast.

"Are the Germans going to throw the captain overboard?" the boy asked.

Dowsey replied that he didn't think they were and the boy said that it was not a difficult task and that he himself could even do it. Dowsey told him that he was not capable of dumping the captain overboard all by himself. The boy said that perhaps the Germans didn't have the gumption to face the captain when he was standing about up on deck and suggested that they smother him in his berth.

This gave Dowsey an idea. He left Stockwell peeling potatoes, left the galley, and went up on deck and spoke with Lambrach at the wheel. In his statement, Dowsey claims, "I spoke to him about the matter, and he said if I went down and stunned the captain he would help me get him out."

Then Dowsey made the move. He grabbed up a metal belaying pin and went down to the captain's cabin. The captain was in his berth. Dowsey swung the belaying pin. Twice he struck the captain on the head—two bloody blows above the ear.

Lambrach went down and peeked into the berth, then summoned Douglas to the scene of the crime. He then told Marlbey what had been done. The mate arrived and told Dowsey to get the captain out. Dowsey asked Douglas if he would do that part of the crime. Douglas said no, he wasn't feeling very well, and he would have Lambrach come down and give Dowsey a hand. Lambrach, however, refused to help, as did Marlbey. Finally Lambrach gave in and helped Dowsey.

As the two culprits struggled to squeeze the captain out of his berth, the poor man pleaded, "Don't my dear men, I will go with you anywhere." Lambrach was in a hurry so they didn't wait to hear more but wrapped the captain in a blanket and dragged him up onto the deck, Dowsey holding his head and Lambrach his feet. At one point Lambrach slipped and fell, and the captain dropped to the deck and repeated what he had said in his berth, but his plea was ignored. Lambrach got back on his feet, and the two men toppled poor Captain Benson over the ship's rail. After he struck the water, he begged, "Save me!"

Dowsey and Bill then went to the forecastle where they found Douglas, who asked, "Did you do it?" even though Dowsey was certain the schemer had watched the entire episode.

They all met in the forecastle and Lambrach clapped his hands and said, "What are we going to do now, we have no captain?"

Douglas, undoubtedly insulted, replied, "What are you talking about? I am captain of the vessel now."

The boy piped in, "The mate is the captain now. You must remember that. You must not call the mate by that name now, but captain."

The sea was dead calm, and they could hear Captain Benson splashing around in the water. They also heard him speak, although from where they stood it sounded like a groan; they were unable to make out what Benson said.

In his statement, Dowsey related what immediately followed:

> The mate asked me how much water we had in the casks. I told him I thought we had enough, if we were going to the West Indies, for the crew we had aboard. He then said he intended to run the vessel close to the American shore, and go ashore in the boat and get a few more men, and he asked me again if I thought we had enough for us and those we were to get. I said I thought that we did; he said we didn't require much, for the wind was fair for the West Indies, and we could run there in eight or nine days. All this time there was nobody at the wheel. He sent Bill [Lambrach] to the wheel, and altered the course of the vessel to the West Indies S.S.W. Up to this time we were on the way to

Boston. After Bill went to the wheel, we all left the forecastle and went on deck. The captain had then got clear of the vessel's stern, and was endeavouring to keep up in the water. I believe had he been able to swim, he would have came on board, but I am certain he had strength to swim if he could. By his motion in the water I judged this. We all stood aft looking at him—the mate was there too. I then thought it was a very wrong thing that had been done. I asked the mate what he thought of it. He then answered that the captain deserved it, for his being nothing but a rogue.

At that moment a schooner came in sight and Douglas was afraid that its crew would see Benson—or the blanket he had been wrapped with—in the water. He found some paint and had Lambrach paint over the name on the stern. Lambrach thought this was a bad move; the schooner might see that the name had been painted out and give them trouble. Fortunately for Douglas and the others, the schooner moved off in another direction and disappeared from view.

The fear of being detected by the schooner over with, Douglas ordered Dowsey to go below and get the ship's papers. At first he couldn't find them, but eventually came across a little box and a bunch of keys. He unlocked the box and found a lot of papers. Being illiterate, he didn't know what they represented, but assumed they were the ship's papers. He also found three shillings and put them in his pocket.

Dowsey took the box up on deck and gave them to Douglas who took out all the papers and examined them with Stockwell's help. Douglas soon announced, "We cannot do as we intended to do." He explained that the *Zero* had "too many papers." The vessel would be missed before they could reach the West Indies, and the authorities would be searching for it. Douglas ordered the boy to burn the papers and the captain's clothes were distributed among the crew.

With no way to steal the *Zero* and its cargo, Douglas decided to scuttle the ship and go to shore in the boat. It was now about four o'clock Sunday afternoon. They planned what they would say if they were questioned: that the captain had been knocked overboard by the jibbing of the boom and they were forced to abandon the ship because it was leaking and they were short handed. The boy was told to keep quiet and send anyone asking questions to the mate.

The boy, Stockwell, later related what happened next:

> It came on dark. At last we saw two lighthouses. The wind died away. We got nearly abreast of the lights. They said it was fit time to sink the ship, and go ashore. The mate told me to go to my room and get one of the large-sized augers. I told him I did not want to go to the cabin, and he sent Charles. Charles brought up the auger and gave it to me. I got into the boat. Charles and the cook were on deck. They tried to chop a hole on the opposite side. They had only one axe between them. The mate and myself were holding the boat to keep her close to the vessel. Bill was boring [holes in the ship]. The sea kept the vessel working a little. On account of the sea the auger broke. Had not bored more than an inch, before the auger broke. It was rusted and dull. The axe flew off the handle, and they could not chop then. Some dispute arose about leaving her. We pulled off and left her. We had then all sails set, except the royal and stay-sail. At this time the cook showed us the captain's watch, and purse with three or four dollars in it. We landed at LaHave Head. We laid down on the grass and went to sleep. This was about three or four o'clock on Friday [*sic*] morning. We had some water and half a barrel of hard-bread. We had blankets with us. It was a rainy morning [Monday, September 11]. I woke up about daylight, 6 o'clock. I saw the Germans go into the bushes. I went to sleep again. It was about nine or ten o'clock when I woke

up again. We thought we were on the mainland. We found that we were on an Island. A fisherman's boat came. We were asked if we were the crew belonging to the brig. This was about twelve o'clock. They asked me and I sent them to see the mate. He told them we had left the brigantine. The fisherman said they had picked up the brigantine. The mate and cook said they did not know anything about the cutting or boring or name being painted out. They said the captain had been knocked overboard by jibing of main boom. The mate said there was six feet of water in the hold when we left her. The fishermen said they did not believe that, as there was but little water in her when they found her. The mate said some vessel must have come across her at sea and painted out the name and cut the hole in her side.

Douglas asked the fishermen where they were and learned that they had landed on Cape LaHave Island, Lunenburg County. They were treated to supper at a fisherman's home and then the fishermen ferried them over to Petite Rivière on the mainland, near the now popular Rissers Beach.

The day after the men landed on the mainland at Petite Rivière, Douglas, Dowsey, and Stockwell were taken into custody and appeared before a magistrate in Liverpool. All three stuck to the same story and were released. But the authorities remained suspicious and ordered an investigation, which resulted in the three men being rearrested. The two Germans, Lambrach and Marlbey had made their way to Liverpool, where they were also apprehended and taken into custody. The trial was held in Halifax and opened on Thursday November 9, 1865.

Both Frank Stockwell and Charles Marlbey testified against John Douglas, Henry Dowsey, and Bill Lambrach, all three of whom were tried for the murder of Captain Benson.

When Douglas appeared for sentencing, he embarked on

a long defence of his actions. "I am perfectly innocent of the crime, of which I have been falsely accused," he announced. He said he didn't hear Dowsey murder the captain as he was asleep at the time. He said he was awakened by Lambrach, and told what had occurred. He went to the captain's cabin and found the cook, Dowsey, "his eyes glaring" standing over Benson's body. He said, "I was paralyzed at the sight and did not know what to do." He said that he left the cabin and was approached by the other German, Charles Marlbey, who requested him to sail the *Zero* to the West Indies. "It flashed on me at once that there was a mutiny," he told the court. "I trembled and thought to my self, 'My turn comes next.'" Of the boy, Stockwell, he exclaimed, "The young rascal was in on the plot."

Douglas told the court that Dowsey requested him to lend a hand in dumping the captain overboard, but he refused to have anything to do with such an outrageous act.

In his extensive testimony, Dowsey made a clean breast of all that had happened and admitted his guilt. He stated that the boy, Stockwell, had said that "It would be a very good thing to watch him when he was in his berth and smother him." Dowsey further stated that the boy had as much to with the murder as the mate had.

There is no indication that the above statements damaged Stockwell's credibility. One newspaper reporter was very much impressed with Stockwell, and wrote, "This boy, who is very intelligent, deserves great credit for the manner in which he gave his testimony, everyone who heard him being impressed with the conviction that he was telling the truth."

John Douglas was sentenced to "life in prison at hard labour." Henry Dowsey was sentenced to be "hung by the neck until dead." William Lambrach was acquitted.

Some four thousand people signed a petition demanding the same sentence for Dowsey as Douglas. Dowsey was a Catholic and Douglas a Baptist, and the petitioners felt that Dowsey was being penalized both because of his religion and his colour. But the government refused to intervene—after all, it was Dowsey who had struck the fatal blow.

Dowsey has gone down in history as the last pirate hanged in Canada.

Glossary

Belaying pin	A removable pin in a ship's rail around which ropes are fastened.
Binnacle	A stand that holds the ship's compass.
Boatswain	A petty officer in charge of a ship's anchors, deck crew, rigging, and cables.
Brigantine	A two-masted vessel with a square-rigged topsail on the mainmast.
Careening	Cleaning, caulking, repairing, etc., a ship's hull while it is leaning or lying on its side, as on a beach.
Careening Grounds	A beach where a ship is hauled in at a low tide and careened.
Galleon	A large sailing ship with high forecastle and stern and three or four masts.
Galley	A long, low ship propelled by oars and sails, usually single-decked.
Gig	A light, two-wheeled carriage pulled by a horse.
Guano	Sea bird manure used as fertilizer. It is found particularly on Peruvian islands.
Impress	To force a person against his or her will into private or public service, especially into a navy.
Jolly Rogers	A black flag with a white skll and cross bones, flown by pirates to try and scare their prey into submission.

Larboard	The left-hand (port) side of a ship looking forward.
Lazarette	Storage space below deck in the stern.
Longboat	A large rowboat carried by a ship, usually equipped with one or more sails to travel long distances at sea.
Man-of-war	An armed naval ship of the colonial era.
Puncheons	Large casks (with capacities ranging from 72 to 120 gallons) for holding wine, rum, beer, etc.
Quadrant	A navigational instrument used to determine a ship's position. Shaped like the quarter section of a circle, it measures the angle of the sun or a star from the horizon.
Ship's papers	Papers carried on a ship giving various amounts of information about the vessel, such as its name, place of registration, owners, and where it was built.
Sloop	A single-masted sailing vessel with a mainsail and jib.
Sun shot	This measures the angle of the sun above the horizon, from a ship, for the purpose of determining the vessel's position. (See **Quadrant**)
Spar	Any pole such as a boom extending from the after side of a mast and supporting a sail.
Tender boat	An auxiliary boat used to ferry crew or passengers to or from a ship near the shore. It's also used to transport food supplies and equipment over short distances.

Weigh anchor	To pull or hoist the anchor.
Whaler	A ship used in fishing whales.
Yards	Slender poles tapered toward the ends, fastened at right angles across masts to support sails.

Bibliography

"Articles on the Zero Case, Nov. 9, Nov. 16, Nov. 23, 1865 and Jan. 25, 1886." Liverpool Transcript, Nova Scotia Archives and Record Management, 2004.

Bowes, James. "Trial of Jones, Hazelton, Anderson and Trevaskiss, alais Johnson, for Piracy and Murder on board barque Saladin." Halifax: printed and sold by James Bowes, 1844.

Bruce, Harry. *An Illustrated History of Nova Scotia*. Halifax: Nimbus Publishing and the Province of Nova Scotia, 1997.

Burns, E. Bradford. *Latin America: A Concise Interpretive History*. New Jersey: Prentice-Hall, Inc., 1972.

Coarse, A. G. *Pirates of Eastern Seas*. Frederick Muller, Ltd., 1966.

Crooker, William S. *Tracking Treasure: In Search of East Coast Bounty*. Halifax: Nimbus Publishing, 1998.

———. *Oak Island Gold*. Halifax: Nimbus Publishing Limited, 1993.

———. *The Oak Island Quest*. Windsor: Lancelot Press, 1978.

Dictionary of National Biography. London, Smith, Elder & Co., England.

Dow, George Francis and John Henry Edmonds. *The Pirates of the New England Coast, 1630-1730*. New York: Dover Publications Inc., 1996.

Eaton, Arthur W. H. *The History of Kings County*. Salem: The Salem Press Company, 1910.

Gosse, Phillip. *The History of Piracy*. New York: Longmans, Green and Co., 1932.

Harris, Reginald V. *The Oak Island Mystery*. Toronto: The Ryerson Press, 1958.

Horwood, Harold. "The Princess and the Pirates," in *Evening Telegram Weekend Magazine*, V. 9, No. 29, July 18, 1959, p9–p12.

McLeod, Carol. *Captain William Kidd: Scapegoat or Scoundrel.* Antigonish: Formac Publishing Company Limited, 1979.

MacMechan, Archibald. *Sagas of the Sea.* New York: E. P. Dutton and Company, 1923.

—————. *At the Harbour Mouth.* Porters Lake, N. S., Portersfield Press, 1988.

More, James F. *The History of Queens County, N. S.* Halifax: Nova Scotia Printing Company, 1873.

Nesmith, Robert L. *Dig for Pirate Treasure.* New York: The Devin-adair Company, 1959.

Newfoundland Historic Trust. *Ten Historic Towns.* St. John's: Newfoundland Historic Trust Publications, Volume 2, 1978.

Prowse, D. W. *A History of Newfoundland.* London: MacMillan, U.K., 1895.

Public Archives of Nova Scotia. "Summary of Judicial Proceedings Related to the Murder of Captain Benson on Board the Brig *Zero.*" Compiled from City Newspapers.

Pyle, Howard. *The Book of Pirates.* New York: Harper & Brothers, 1921.

Raddall, Thomas H. *Footsteps on Old Floors.* Porters Lake, NS: Portersfield Press, reprinted 2001.

Ritchie, Robert C. *Captain Kidd and the War Against Pirates.* Cambridge, Massachusetts: Harvard University Press, 1986.

Sherwood, Ronald H. *Legends, Oddities and Facts from the Maritime Provinces.* Hantsport, NS: Lancelot Press, 1984.

—————. *Sagas of the Land and Sea.* Hantsport, NS: Lancelot Press, 1980.

—————. *Secrets of the North Atlantic Islands.* New York: Dodd, Mead and Company, 1950.

Snow, Edward Rowe. *True Tales of Pirates and Their Gold.* New York: Mead and Company, 1963.

"Trial of Jordan and his Wife." *Quebec Gazette,* No.2336, January 25, 1810.

Wells, H. G. *The Outline of History.* New York: Doubleday & Company, Inc., 1961.

Winston, Alexander. *No Man Knows My Grave: Privateers and Pirates, 1665–1715.* Boston: Houghton Miffin Company, 1969.